MznLnx

Missing Links Exam Preps

Exam Prep for

Operations Management Meeting Customers' Demands

Knod, Schonberger, 7th Edition

The MznLnx Exam Prep is your link from the texbook and lecture to your exams.
The MznLnx Exam Preps are unauthorized and comprehensive reviews of your textbooks.

All material provided by MznLnx and Rico Publications (c) 2010
Textbook publishers and textbook authors do not particpate in or contribute to these reviews.

MznLnx

Rico
Publications

Exam Prep for Operations Management Meeting Customers' Demands
7th Edition
Knod, Schonberger

Publisher: Raymond Houge
Assistant Editor: Michael Rouger
Text and Cover Designer: Lisa Buckner
Marketing Manager: Sara Swagger
Project Manager, Editorial Production: Jerry Emerson
Art Director: Vernon Lowerui

Product Manager: Dave Mason
Editorial Assitant: Rachel Guzmanji
Pedagogy: Debra Long
Cover Image: Jim Reed/Getty Images
Text and Cover Printer: City Printing, Inc.
Compositor: Media Mix, Inc.

(c) 2010 Rico Publications
ALL RIGHTS RESERVED. No part of this work covered by the copyright may be reproduced or used in any form or by an means--graphic, electronic, or mechanical, including photocopying, recording, taping, Web distribution, information storage, and retrieval systems, or in any other manner--without the written permission of the publisher.

Printed in the United States
ISBN:

For more information about our products, contact us at:
Dave.Mason@RicoPublications.com

For permission to use material from this text or product, submit a request online to:
Dave.Mason@RicoPublications.com

Contents

CHAPTER 1
Operations Management: Introductory Concepts 1

CHAPTER 2
OM Strategy: Dynamic Competitiveness 8

CHAPTER 3
Principles of Operations Management 18

CHAPTER 4
Demand Management and Forecasting 24

CHAPTER 5
Capacity Planning and Master Scheduling 30

CHAPTER 6
Order Fulfillment and Purchasing 33

CHAPTER 7
Designing for Customers' Needs 42

CHAPTER 8
The Quality Imperative 52

CHAPTER 9
Process Control and Improvement 63

CHAPTER 10
Flow-Control: Eliminating Process Waste 71

CHAPTER 11
Timing-Another Imperative 79

CHAPTER 12
People Demand Productivity 84

CHAPTER 13
Managing Materials: Timing and Quantities 92

CHAPTER 14
Facilities Management 104

CHAPTER 15
Managing Continuous and Repetitive Operations 108

CHAPTER 16
Managing Job and Batch Operations 111

CHAPTER 17
Managing Projects 117

ANSWER KEY 127

TO THE STUDENT

COMPREHENSIVE

The *MznLnx* Exam Prep series is designed to help you pass your exams. Editors at MznLnx review your textbooks and then prepare these practice exams to help you master the textbook material. Unlike study guides, workbooks, and practice tests provided by the texbook publisher and textbook authors, *MznLnx* gives you **all** of the material in each chapter in exam form, not just samples, so you can be sure to nail your exam.

MECHANICAL

The MznLnx Exam Prep series creates exams that will help you learn the subject matter as well as test you on your understanding. Each question is designed to help you master the concept. Just working through the exams, you gain an understanding of the subject--its a simple mechanical process that produces success.

INTEGRATED STUDY GUIDE AND REVIEW

MznLnx is not just a set of exams designed to test you, its also a comprehensive review of the subject content. Each exam question is also a review of the concept, making sure that you will get the answer correct without having to go to other sources of material. You learn as you go! Its the easiest way to pass an exam.

HUMOR

Studying can be tedious and dry. MznLnx's instructional design includes moderate humor within the exam questions on occassion, to break the tedium and revitalize the brain

Chapter 1. Operations Management: Introductory Concepts

1. _____ is an area of business concerned with the production of goods and services, and involves the responsibility of ensuring that business operations are efficient in terms of using as little resource as needed, and effective in terms of meeting customer requirements. It is concerned with managing the process that converts inputs (in the forms of materials, labour and energy) into outputs (in the form of goods and services.)

Operations traditionally refers to the production of goods and services separately, although the distinction between these two main types of operations is increasingly difficult to make as manufacturers tend to merge product and service offerings.

   a. A4e
   b. A Stake in the Outcome
   c. AAAI
   d. Operations management

2. _____ is a term defined by the Oxford English Dictionary as an individual's 'course or progress through life '. It is usually considered to pertain to remunerative work (and sometimes also formal education.)

The etymology of the term is somewhat ironic in that it comes from the Latin word carrera, which means race .

   a. Career
   b. Career planning
   c. Spatial mismatch
   d. Nursing shortage

3. _____ refers to the difference between the cost of materials purchased by a company plus the cost of the labor to assemble a product and the price at which the company sells the product. An example is the price of gasoline at the pump over the price of the oil in it. In national accounts used in macroeconomics, it refers to the contribution of the factors of production, i.e., land, labor, and capital goods, to raising the value of a product and corresponds to the incomes received by the owners of these factors.
   a. Minimum wage
   b. Rehn-Meidner Model
   c. Deregulation
   d. Value added

4. A _____ is a list of the general tasks and responsibilities of a position. Typically, it also includes to whom the position reports, specifications such as the qualifications needed by the person in the job, salary range for the position, etc. A _____ is usually developed by conducting a job analysis, which includes examining the tasks and sequences of tasks necessary to perform the job.

a. Recruitment advertising
b. Recruitment Process Insourcing
c. Recruitment
d. Job description

5. _____ is an advertisement in which a particular product specifically mentions a competitor by name for the express purpose of showing why the competitor is inferior to the product naming it.

This should not be confused with parody advertisements, where a fictional product is being advertised for the purpose of poking fun at the particular advertisement, nor should it be confused with the use of a coined brand name for the purpose of comparing the product without actually naming an actual competitor. ('Wikipedia tastes better and is less filling than the Encyclopedia Galactica.')

In the 1980s, during what has been referred to as the cola wars, soft-drink manufacturer Pepsi ran a series of advertisements where people, caught on hidden camera, in a blind taste test, chose Pepsi over rival Coca-Cola.

a. 1990 Clean Air Act
b. 33 Strategies of War
c. Comparative advertising
d. 28-hour day

6. An _____ is a manufacturing process in which parts (usually interchangeable parts) are added to a product in a sequential manner using optimally planned logistics to create a finished product much faster than with handcrafting-type methods. The _____ developed by Ford Motor Company between 1908 and 1915 made _____s famous in the following decade through the social ramifications of mass production, such as the affordability of the Ford Model T and the introduction of high wages for Ford workers. However, the various preconditions for the development at Ford stretched far back into the 19th century, from the gradual realization of the dream of interchangeability, to the concept of reinventing workflow and job descriptions using analytical methods.

a. AAAI
b. A4e
c. A Stake in the Outcome
d. Assembly line

7. In probability theory, a probability distribution is called _____ if its cumulative distribution function is _____. This is equivalent to saying that for random variables X with the distribution in question, Pr[X = a] = 0 for all real numbers a, i.e.: the probability that X attains the value a is zero, for any number a. If the distribution of X is _____ then X is called a _____ random variable.

a. Connectionist expert systems
b. Decision tree pruning
c. Pay Band
d. Continuous

8. _____ refers to the movement of cash into or out of a business or financial product. It is usually measured during a specified, finite period of time. Measurement of _____ can be used

- to determine a project's rate of return or value. The time of _____s into and out of projects are used as inputs in financial models such as internal rate of return, and net present value.
- to determine problems with a business's liquidity. Being profitable does not necessarily mean being liquid. A company can fail because of a shortage of cash, even while profitable.
- as an alternate measure of a business's profits when it is believed that accrual accounting concepts do not represent economic realities. For example, a company may be notionally profitable but generating little operational cash (as may be the case for a company that barters its products rather than selling for cash.) In such a case, the company may be deriving additional operating cash by issuing shares evaluating default risk, re-investment requirements, etc.

_____ is a generic term used differently depending on the context. It may be defined by users for their own purposes.

a. Sweat equity
b. Cash flow
c. Gross profit
d. Gross profit margin

9. _____ is execution of a series of programs ('jobs') on a computer without human interaction.

Batch jobs are set up so they can be run to completion without human interaction, so all input data is preselected through scripts or command-line parameters. This is in contrast to 'online' or interactive programs which prompt the user for such input.

a. 1990 Clean Air Act
b. 28-hour day
c. 33 Strategies of War
d. Batch processing

10. A _____ is the period of time between the initiation of any process of production and the completion of that process. Thus the _____ for ordering a new car from a manufacturer may be anywhere from 2 weeks to 6 months. In industry, _____ reduction is an important part of lean manufacturing.

a. 33 Strategies of War
b. 28-hour day
c. Lead time
d. 1990 Clean Air Act

11. In economics, business, retail, and accounting, a _____ is the value of money that has been used up to produce something, and hence is not available for use anymore. In economics, a _____ is an alternative that is given up as a result of a decision. In business, the _____ may be one of acquisition, in which case the amount of money expended to acquire it is counted as _____.
   a. Cost
   b. Fixed costs
   c. Cost overrun
   d. Cost allocation

12. _____ is the provision of service to customers before, during and after a purchase.

According to Turban et al. (2002), '_____ is a series of activities designed to enhance the level of customer satisfaction - that is, the feeling that a product or service has met the customer expectation.'

Its importance varies by product, industry and customer; defective or broken merchandise can be exchanged, often only with a receipt and within a specified time frame.

   a. 1990 Clean Air Act
   b. Customer service
   c. 28-hour day
   d. Service rate

13. The _____ is given by the United States National Institute of Standards and Technology. Through the actions of the National Productivity Advisory Committee chaired by Jack Grayson, it was established by the Malcolm Baldrige National Quality Improvement Act of 1987 - Public Law 100-107 and named for Malcolm Baldrige, who served as United States Secretary of Commerce during the Reagan administration from 1981 until his 1987 death in a rodeo accident. APQC, , organized the first White House Conference on Productivity, spearheading the creation and design of the _____ in 1987, and jointly administering the award for its first three years.
   a. Malcolm Baldrige National Quality Award
   b. Business Network Transformation
   c. Time and attendance
   d. Scenario planning

14. A _____ is a group of employees from various functional areas of the organization - research, engineering, marketing, finance. human resources, and operations, for example - who are all focused on a specific objective and are responsible to work as a team to improve coordination and innovation across divisions and resolve mutual problems.
   a. Graduate recruitment
   b. Sociotechnical systems
   c. Cross-functional team
   d. Goal-setting theory

15. A _____ is the system of organizations, people, technology, activities, information and resources involved in moving a product or service from supplier to customer. _____ activities transform natural resources, raw materials and components into a finished product that is delivered to the end customer. In sophisticated _____ systems, used products may re-enter the _____ at any point where residual value is recyclable.
   a. Drop shipping
   b. Wholesalers
   c. Supply chain
   d. Packaging

16. _____ is the management of a network of interconnected businesses involved in the ultimate provision of product and service packages required by end customers (Harland, 1996.) _____ spans all movement and storage of raw materials, work-in-process inventory, and finished goods from point of origin to point of consumption (supply chain.)

The definition an American professional association put forward is that _____ encompasses the planning and management of all activities involved in sourcing, procurement, conversion, and logistics management activities.

   a. Packaging
   b. Drop shipping
   c. Freight forwarder
   d. Supply chain management

17. The _____ is a concept from business management that was first described and popularized by Michael Porter in his 1985 best-seller, Competitive Advantage: Creating and Sustaining Superior Performance.

A _____ is a chain of activities. Products pass through all activities of the chain in order and at each activity the product gains some value. The chain of activities gives the products more added value than the sum of added values of all activities. It is important not to mix the concept of the _____ with the costs occurring throughout the activities.

a. Customer relationship management
b. Market development
c. Value chain
d. Mass marketing

18. _____, a business term, is a measure of how products and services supplied by a company meet or surpass customer expectation. It is seen as a key performance indicator within business and is part of the four perspectives of a Balanced Scorecard.

In a competitive marketplace where businesses compete for customers, _____ is seen as a key differentiator and increasingly has become a key element of business strategy.

a. Horizontal integration
b. Critical Success Factor
c. Foreign ownership
d. Customer Satisfaction

19. In economics, _____ is the desire to own something and the ability to pay for it. The term _____ signifies the ability or the willingness to buy a particular commodity at a given point of time.
a. Demand
b. 33 Strategies of War
c. 1990 Clean Air Act
d. 28-hour day

20. _____ is the activity of estimating the quantity of a product or service that consumers will purchase. _____ involves techniques including both informal methods, such as educated guesses, and quantitative methods, such as the use of historical sales data or current data from test markets. _____ may be used in making pricing decisions, in assessing future capacity requirements, or in making decisions on whether to enter a new market.
a. 28-hour day
b. Profitability index
c. 1990 Clean Air Act
d. Demand forecasting

21. _____ is the process of estimation in unknown situations. Prediction is a similar, but more general term. Both can refer to estimation of time series, cross-sectional or longitudinal data.

a. 33 Strategies of War
b. 28-hour day
c. Forecasting
d. 1990 Clean Air Act

22. _____ refers to metrics and measures of output from production processes, per unit of input. Labor _____, for example, is typically measured as a ratio of output per labor-hour, an input. _____ may be conceived of as a metrics of the technical or engineering efficiency of production.
   a. Value engineering
   b. Remanufacturing
   c. Productivity
   d. Master production schedule

Chapter 2. OM Strategy: Dynamic Competitiveness

1. In probability theory, a probability distribution is called _____ if its cumulative distribution function is _____. This is equivalent to saying that for random variables X with the distribution in question, Pr[X = a] = 0 for all real numbers a, i.e.: the probability that X attains the value a is zero, for any number a. If the distribution of X is _____ then X is called a _____ random variable.
   a. Connectionist expert systems
   b. Continuous
   c. Decision tree pruning
   d. Pay Band

2. _____ is a management process whereby delivery (customer valued) processes are constantly evaluated and improved in the light of their efficiency, effectiveness and flexibility.

   Some see it as a meta process for most management systems (Business Process Management, Quality Management, Project Management). Deming saw it as part of the 'system' whereby feedback from the process and customer were evaluated against organisational goals.

   a. Sole proprietorship
   b. First-mover advantage
   c. Critical Success Factor
   d. Continuous Improvement Process

3. _____ is a Japanese philosophy that focuses on continuous improvement throughout all aspects of life. When applied to the workplace, _____ activities continually improve all functions of a business, from manufacturing to management and from the CEO to the assembly line workers. By improving standardized activities and processes, _____ aims to eliminate waste.
   a. Cross-docking
   b. Psychological pricing
   c. Kaizen
   d. Sensitivity analysis

4. _____ or lean production, which is often known simply as 'Lean', is a production practice that considers the expenditure of resources for any goal other than the creation of value for the end customer to be wasteful, and thus a target for elimination. Working from the perspective of the customer who consumes a product or service, 'value' is defined as any action or process that a customer would be willing to pay for. Basically, lean is centered around creating more value with less work.
   a. Production line
   b. Theory of constraints
   c. Six Sigma
   d. Lean manufacturing

5. A _____ is a computer program typically used to provide some form of artificial intelligence, which consists primarily of a set of rules about behavior. These rules, termed productions, are a basic representation found useful in AI planning, expert systems and action selection. A _____ provides the mechanism necessary to execute productions in order to achieve some goal for the system.
   a. 1990 Clean Air Act
   b. 33 Strategies of War
   c. 28-hour day
   d. Production system

6. _____ is a business management strategy aimed at embedding awareness of quality in all organizational processes. _____ has been widely used in manufacturing, education, hospitals, call centers, government, and service industries, as well as NASA space and science programs.

As defined by the International Organization for Standardization (ISO):

> '_____ is a management approach for an organization, centered on quality, based on the participation of all its members and aiming at long-term success through customer satisfaction, and benefits to all members of the organization and to society.' ISO 8402:1994

One major aim is to reduce variation from every process so that greater consistency of effort is obtained. (Royse, D., Thyer, B., Padgett D., ' Logan T., 2006)

   a. 28-hour day
   b. 1990 Clean Air Act
   c. Total quality management
   d. Quality management

7. _____ can be considered to have three main components: quality control, quality assurance and quality improvement. _____ is focused not only on product quality, but also the means to achieve it. _____ therefore uses quality assurance and control of processes as well as products to achieve more consistent quality.
   a. Total quality management
   b. 28-hour day
   c. 1990 Clean Air Act
   d. Quality management

8. In marketing, _____ is the process of distinguishing the differences of a product or offering from others, to make it more attractive to a particular target market. This involves differentiating it from competitors' products as well as one's own product offerings.

a. PEST analysis
b. Market development
c. Market share
d. Product differentiation

9. _____ is an advertisement in which a particular product specifically mentions a competitor by name for the express purpose of showing why the competitor is inferior to the product naming it.

This should not be confused with parody advertisements, where a fictional product is being advertised for the purpose of poking fun at the particular advertisement, nor should it be confused with the use of a coined brand name for the purpose of comparing the product without actually naming an actual competitor. ('Wikipedia tastes better and is less filling than the Encyclopedia Galactica.')

In the 1980s, during what has been referred to as the cola wars, soft-drink manufacturer Pepsi ran a series of advertisements where people, caught on hidden camera, in a blind taste test, chose Pepsi over rival Coca-Cola.

a. 28-hour day
b. 33 Strategies of War
c. 1990 Clean Air Act
d. Comparative advertising

10. _____ is an area of business concerned with the production of goods and services, and involves the responsibility of ensuring that business operations are efficient in terms of using as little resource as needed, and effective in terms of meeting customer requirements. It is concerned with managing the process that converts inputs (in the forms of materials, labour and energy) into outputs (in the form of goods and services.)

Operations traditionally refers to the production of goods and services separately, although the distinction between these two main types of operations is increasingly difficult to make as manufacturers tend to merge product and service offerings.

a. A Stake in the Outcome
b. AAAI
c. A4e
d. Operations management

11. The _____ was a period in the late 18th and early 19th centuries when major changes in agriculture, manufacturing, mining, and transportation had a profound effect on the socioeconomic and cultural conditions in Britain. The changes subsequently spread throughout Europe, North America, and eventually the world. The onset of the _____ marked a major turning point in human society; almost every aspect of daily life was eventually influenced in some way.

a. Industrial Revolution
b. Adam Smith
c. Affiliation
d. Abraham Harold Maslow

12. _____ is a theory of management that analyzes and synthesizes workflows, with the objective of improving labour productivity. The core ideas of the theory were developed by Frederick Winslow Taylor in the 1880s and 1890s, and were first published in his monographs, Shop Management and The Principles of _____ Taylor believed that decisions based upon tradition and rules of thumb should be replaced by precise procedures developed after careful study of an individual at work.

a. Master production schedule
b. Value engineering
c. Capacity planning
d. Scientific management

13. _____ is an effective method of monitoring a process through the use of control charts. Control charts enable the use of objective criteria for distinguishing background variation from events of significance based on statistical techniques. Much of its power lies in the ability to monitor both process center and its variation about that center.

a. Single Minute Exchange of Die
b. Quality control
c. Statistical process control
d. Process capability

14. _____, widely known as F. W. Taylor, was an American mechanical engineer who sought to improve industrial efficiency. He is regarded as the father of scientific management, and was one of the first management consultants.

Taylor was one of the intellectual leaders of the Efficiency Movement and his ideas, broadly conceived, were highly influential in the Progressive Era.

a. Jonah Jacob Goldberg
b. Frederick Winslow Taylor
c. Douglas N. Daft
d. Geoffrey Colvin

15. _____ is one of the managerial functions like planning, organizing, staffing and directing. It is an important function because it helps to check the errors and to take the corrective action so that deviation from standards are minimized and stated goals of the organization are achieved in desired manner. According to modern concepts, _____ is a foreseeing action whereas earlier concept of _____ was used only when errors were detected. _____ in management means setting standards, measuring actual performance and taking corrective action.
   a. Decision tree pruning
   b. Control
   c. Turnover
   d. Schedule of reinforcement

16. _____ is a software based production planning and inventory control system used to manage manufacturing processes. Although it is not common nowadays, it is possible to conduct _____ by hand as well.

An _____ system is intended to simultaneously meet three objectives:

- Ensure materials and products are available for production and delivery to customers.
- Maintain the lowest possible level of inventory.
- Plan manufacturing activities, delivery schedules and purchasing activities.

Manufacturing organizations, whatever their products, face the same daily practical problem - that customers want products to be available in a shorter time than it takes to make them. This means that some level of planning is required.

   a. 1990 Clean Air Act
   b. 28-hour day
   c. 33 Strategies of War
   d. Material requirements planning

17. _____ refers to the difference between the cost of materials purchased by a company plus the cost of the labor to assemble a product and the price at which the company sells the product. An example is the price of gasoline at the pump over the price of the oil in it. In national accounts used in macroeconomics, it refers to the contribution of the factors of production, i.e., land, labor, and capital goods, to raising the value of a product and corresponds to the incomes received by the owners of these factors.
   a. Minimum wage
   b. Rehn-Meidner Model
   c. Deregulation
   d. Value added

18. _____ is a term defined by the Oxford English Dictionary as an individual's 'course or progress through life '. It is usually considered to pertain to remunerative work (and sometimes also formal education.)

The etymology of the term is somewhat ironic in that it comes from the Latin word carrera, which means race .

a. Career planning
b. Nursing shortage
c. Career
d. Spatial mismatch

19. In economics, business, retail, and accounting, a _____ is the value of money that has been used up to produce something, and hence is not available for use anymore. In economics, a _____ is an alternative that is given up as a result of a decision. In business, the _____ may be one of acquisition, in which case the amount of money expended to acquire it is counted as _____.

a. Fixed costs
b. Cost
c. Cost allocation
d. Cost overrun

20. In economics ' business, specifically cost accounting, the _____ is the point at which cost or expenses and revenue are equal: there is no net loss or gain, and one has 'broken even'. A profit or a loss has not been made, although opportunity costs have been paid, and capital has received the risk-adjusted, expected return.

For example, if the business sells less than 200 tables each month, it will make a loss, if it sells more, it will be a profit.

a. Virtuous circle
b. Defined benefit pension plan
c. Fixed asset turnover
d. Break-even point

21. In economics, _____ are business expenses that are not dependent on the activities of the business They tend to be time-related, such as salaries or rents being paid per month. This is in contrast to variable costs, which are volume-related (and are paid per quantity.)

In management accounting, _____ are defined as expenses that do not change in proportion to the activity of a business, within the relevant period or scale of production.

Chapter 2. OM Strategy: Dynamic Competitiveness

a. Fixed costs
b. Transaction cost
c. Cost allocation
d. Cost of quality

22. In cost-volume-profit analysis, a form of management accounting, _____ is the marginal profit per unit sale. It is a useful quantity in carrying out various calculations, and can be used as a measure of operating leverage.

The Total _____ is Total Revenue (TR, or Sales) minus Total Variable Cost (TVC):

    TContribution margin = TR − TVC

The Unit _____ (C) is Unit Revenue (Price, P) minus Unit Variable Cost (V):

    C = P − V

The _____ Ratio is the percentage of Contribution over Total Revenue, which can be calculated from the unit contribution over unit price or total contribution over Total Revenue:

$$\frac{C}{P} = \frac{P-V}{P} = \frac{\text{Unit Contribution Margin}}{\text{Price}} = \frac{\text{Total Contribution Margin}}{\text{Total Revenue}}$$

For instance, if the price is $10 and the unit variable cost is $2, then the unit _____ is $8, and the _____ ratio is $8/$10 = 80%.

a. Factory overhead
b. Customer profitability
c. Profit center
d. Contribution margin

23. _____, commonly known as e-commerce, consists of the buying and selling of products or services over electronic systems such as the Internet and other computer networks. The amount of trade conducted electronically has grown extraordinarily with widespread Internet usage. The use of commerce is conducted in this way, spurring and drawing on innovations in electronic funds transfer, supply chain management, Internet marketing, online transaction processing, electronic data interchange (EDI), inventory management systems, and automated data collection systems.

a. Online shopping
b. A Stake in the Outcome
c. A4e
d. Electronic Commerce

24. _____ is the amount of goods and services that a labourer produces in a given amount of time. It is one of several types of productivity that economists measure. _____ can be measured for a firm, a process or a country.
   a. Business Network Transformation
   b. Time and attendance
   c. Retroactive overtime
   d. Labour productivity

25. _____ refers to metrics and measures of output from production processes, per unit of input. Labor _____, for example, is typically measured as a ratio of output per labor-hour, an input. _____ may be conceived of as a metrics of the technical or engineering efficiency of production.
   a. Value engineering
   b. Remanufacturing
   c. Master production schedule
   d. Productivity

26. _____ describes commerce transactions between businesses, such as between a manufacturer and a wholesaler, or between a wholesaler and a retailer. Contrasting terms are business-to-consumer (B2C) and business-to-government (B2G.)

The volume of B2B transactions is much higher than the volume of B2C transactions.

   a. Market environment
   b. Product bundling
   c. Business-to-business
   d. Category management

27. An _____ is typically a company that uses a component made by a second company in its own product or sells the product of the second company under its own brand. The specific meaning of the term varies in different contexts.
   a. A Stake in the Outcome
   b. Original equipment manufacturer
   c. AAAI
   d. A4e

28. A _____ is a type of business entity in which partners (owners) share with each other the profits or losses of the business. _____s are often favored over corporations for taxation purposes, as the _____ structure does not generally incur a tax on profits before it is distributed to the partners (i.e. there is no dividend tax levied.) However, depending on the _____ structure and the jurisdiction in which it operates, owners of a _____ may be exposed to greater personal liability than they would as shareholders of a corporation.

a. Due process
b. Mediation
c. Federal Employers Liability Act
d. Partnership

29. _____ is something that a firm can do well and that meets the following three conditions:

Competencies are things that companys execute well across several business units or product sectors.

Firms usually have few competencies, but these are usually less liable to change rapidly.

1. It provides consumer benefits
2. It is not easy for competitors to imitate
3. It can be leveraged widely to many products and markets.

A _____ can take various forms, including technical/subject matter know-how, a reliable process and/or close relationships with customers and suppliers (Mascarenhas et al. 1998.)

a. Learning-by-doing
b. Dominant Design
c. NAIRU
d. Core competency

30. _____ is subcontracting a process, such as product design or manufacturing, to a third-party company. The decision to outsource is often made in the interest of lowering cost or making better use of time and energy costs, redirecting or conserving energy directed at the competencies of a particular business, or to make more efficient use of land, labor, capital, (information) technology and resources. _____ became part of the business lexicon during the 1980s.

a. Opinion leadership
b. Unemployment insurance
c. Outsourcing
d. Operant conditioning

31. The _____ Automobile Company is an automobile manufacturer based in Wolfsburg, Germany, and is the original brand within the _____ Group, as well as the largest brand by sales volume.

_____ means 'people's car' in German, in which it is pronounced . Its current tagline or slogan is Das Auto .

a. Competence-based Strategic Management
b. Rate of return
c. Turnover
d. Volkswagen

Chapter 3. Principles of Operations Management

1. _____ is an area of business concerned with the production of goods and services, and involves the responsibility of ensuring that business operations are efficient in terms of using as little resource as needed, and effective in terms of meeting customer requirements. It is concerned with managing the process that converts inputs (in the forms of materials, labour and energy) into outputs (in the form of goods and services.)

Operations traditionally refers to the production of goods and services separately, although the distinction between these two main types of operations is increasingly difficult to make as manufacturers tend to merge product and service offerings.

   a. A Stake in the Outcome
   b. AAAI
   c. Operations management
   d. A4e

2. _____ is a term defined by the Oxford English Dictionary as an individual's 'course or progress through life '. It is usually considered to pertain to remunerative work (and sometimes also formal education.)

The etymology of the term is somewhat ironic in that it comes from the Latin word carrera, which means race .

   a. Career planning
   b. Spatial mismatch
   c. Career
   d. Nursing shortage

3. A _____ is the period of time between the initiation of any process of production and the completion of that process. Thus the _____ for ordering a new car from a manufacturer may be anywhere from 2 weeks to 6 months. In industry, _____ reduction is an important part of lean manufacturing.

   a. 33 Strategies of War
   b. 28-hour day
   c. Lead time
   d. 1990 Clean Air Act

4. _____ is the process of comparing the cost, cycle time, productivity, or quality of a specific process or method to another that is widely considered to be an industry standard or best practice. Essentially, _____ provides a snapshot of the performance of your business and helps you understand where you are in relation to a particular standard. The result is often a business case for making changes in order to make improvements.

Chapter 3. Principles of Operations Management

a. Cost leadership
b. Complementors
c. Competitive heterogeneity
d. Benchmarking

5. In probability theory, a probability distribution is called _____ if its cumulative distribution function is _____. This is equivalent to saying that for random variables X with the distribution in question, Pr[X = a] = 0 for all real numbers a, i.e.: the probability that X attains the value a is zero, for any number a. If the distribution of X is _____ then X is called a _____ random variable.

a. Continuous
b. Pay Band
c. Connectionist expert systems
d. Decision tree pruning

6. _____ is a management process whereby delivery (customer valued) processes are constantly evaluated and improved in the light of their efficiency, effectiveness and flexibility.

Some see it as a meta process for most management systems (Business Process Management, Quality Management, Project Management). Deming saw it as part of the 'system' whereby feedback from the process and customer were evaluated against organisational goals.

a. Continuous Improvement Process
b. Critical Success Factor
c. First-mover advantage
d. Sole proprietorship

7. _____ is the provision of service to customers before, during and after a purchase.

According to Turban et al. (2002), '_____ is a series of activities designed to enhance the level of customer satisfaction - that is, the feeling that a product or service has met the customer expectation.'

Its importance varies by product, industry and customer; defective or broken merchandise can be exchanged, often only with a receipt and within a specified time frame.

a. Service rate
b. 1990 Clean Air Act
c. 28-hour day
d. Customer service

Chapter 3. Principles of Operations Management

8. The _____ is given by the United States National Institute of Standards and Technology. Through the actions of the National Productivity Advisory Committee chaired by Jack Grayson, it was established by the Malcolm Baldrige National Quality Improvement Act of 1987 - Public Law 100-107 and named for Malcolm Baldrige, who served as United States Secretary of Commerce during the Reagan administration from 1981 until his 1987 death in a rodeo accident. APQC, , organized the first White House Conference on Productivity, spearheading the creation and design of the _____ in 1987, and jointly administering the award for its first three years.

   a. Time and attendance
   b. Business Network Transformation
   c. Scenario planning
   d. Malcolm Baldrige National Quality Award

9. _____ is an advertisement in which a particular product specifically mentions a competitor by name for the express purpose of showing why the competitor is inferior to the product naming it.

This should not be confused with parody advertisements, where a fictional product is being advertised for the purpose of poking fun at the particular advertisement, nor should it be confused with the use of a coined brand name for the purpose of comparing the product without actually naming an actual competitor. ('Wikipedia tastes better and is less filling than the Encyclopedia Galactica.')

In the 1980s, during what has been referred to as the cola wars, soft-drink manufacturer Pepsi ran a series of advertisements where people, caught on hidden camera, in a blind taste test, chose Pepsi over rival Coca-Cola.

   a. 1990 Clean Air Act
   b. 28-hour day
   c. 33 Strategies of War
   d. Comparative advertising

10. _____ refers to training in different ways to improve overall performance. It takes advantage of the particular effectiveness of each training method, while at the same time attempting to neglect the shortcomings of that method by combining it with other methods that address its weaknesses.

Cross training is employee-employer field means, training employees to do one another's work.

   a. 1990 Clean Air Act
   b. 28-hour day
   c. Cross-training
   d. 33 Strategies of War

Chapter 3. Principles of Operations Management 21

11. _____ is an increasingly broadening term with which an organization, or other human system describes the combination of traditionally administrative personnel functions with acquisition and application of skills, knowledge and experience, Employee Relations and resource planning at various levels. The field draws upon concepts developed in Industrial/Organizational Psychology and System Theory. _____ has at least two related interpretations depending on context. The original usage derives from political economy and economics, where it was traditionally called labor, one of four factors of production although this perspective is changing as a function of new and ongoing research into more strategic approaches at national levels. This first usage is used more in terms of '_____ development', and can go beyond just organizations to the level of nations . The more traditional usage within corporations and businesses refers to the individuals within a firm or agency, and to the portion of the organization that deals with hiring, firing, training, and other personnel issues, typically referred to as `_____ management'.

   a. Human resources
   b. Progressive discipline
   c. Human resource management
   d. Bradford Factor

12. _____ is an approach to management development where an individual is moved through a schedule of assignments designed to give him or her a breadth of exposure to the entire operation.

   _____ is also practiced to allow qualified employees to gain more insights into the processes of a company, and to reduce boredom and increase job satisfaction through job variation.

   The term _____ can also mean the scheduled exchange of persons in offices, especially in public offices, prior to the end of incumbency or the legislative period.

   a. 1990 Clean Air Act
   b. 28-hour day
   c. 33 Strategies of War
   d. Job rotation

13. _____ is the use of control systems (such as numerical control, programmable logic control, and other industrial control systems), in concert with other applications of information technology (such as computer-aided technologies [CAD, CAM, CAx]), to control industrial machinery and processes, reducing the need for human intervention. In the scope of industrialization, _____ is a step beyond mechanization. Whereas mechanization provided human operators with machinery to assist them with the physical requirements of work, _____ greatly reduces the need for human sensory and mental requirements as well.

   a. A4e
   b. AAAI
   c. A Stake in the Outcome
   d. Automation

Chapter 3. Principles of Operations Management

14. The metastability in flip-flops can be avoided by ensuring that the data and control inputs are held valid and constant for specified periods before and after the clock pulse, called the _____ and the hold time (t_h) respectively. These times are specified in the data sheet for the device, and are typically between a few nanoseconds and a few hundred picoseconds for modern devices.

Unfortunately, it is not always possible to meet the setup and hold criteria, because the flip-flop may be connected to a real-time signal that could change at any time, outside the control of the designer.

   a. 33 Strategies of War
   b. 1990 Clean Air Act
   c. 28-hour day
   d. Setup time

15. In economics and related disciplines, a _____ is a cost incurred in making an economic exchange. For example, most people, when buying or selling a stock, must pay a commission to their broker; that commission is a _____ of doing the stock deal. Or consider buying a banana from a store; to purchase the banana, your costs will be not only the price of the banana itself, but also the energy and effort it requires to find out which of the various banana products you prefer, where to get them and at what price, the cost of traveling from your house to the store and back, the time waiting in line, and the effort of the paying itself; the costs above and beyond the cost of the banana are the _____s.
   a. Cost accounting
   b. Fixed costs
   c. Cost overrun
   d. Transaction cost

16. In economics, business, retail, and accounting, a _____ is the value of money that has been used up to produce something, and hence is not available for use anymore. In economics, a _____ is an alternative that is given up as a result of a decision. In business, the _____ may be one of acquisition, in which case the amount of money expended to acquire it is counted as _____.
   a. Fixed costs
   b. Cost overrun
   c. Cost allocation
   d. Cost

17. _____ is a manufacturing process for producing parts from both thermoplastic and thermosetting plastic materials. Material is fed into a heated barrel, mixed, and forced into a mold cavity where it cools and hardens to the configuration of the mold cavity. After a product is designed, usually by an industrial designer or an engineer, molds are made by a moldmaker from metal, usually either steel or aluminium, and precision-machined to form the features of the desired part.

a. A4e
b. AAAI
c. A Stake in the Outcome
d. Injection molding

Chapter 4. Demand Management and Forecasting

1. In economics, _____ is the desire to own something and the ability to pay for it. The term _____ signifies the ability or the willingness to buy a particular commodity at a given point of time.
   a. Demand
   b. 28-hour day
   c. 33 Strategies of War
   d. 1990 Clean Air Act

2. In economics, _____' is the art or science of controlling economic demand to avoid a recession. In natural resources management and environmental policy more generally, it refers to policies to control consumer demand for environmentally sensitive or harmful goods such as water and energy. Within manufacturing firms the term is used to describe the activities of demand forecasting, planning and order fulfillment.
   a. 33 Strategies of War
   b. 28-hour day
   c. 1990 Clean Air Act
   d. Demand management

3. _____ is the activity of estimating the quantity of a product or service that consumers will purchase. _____ involves techniques including both informal methods, such as educated guesses, and quantitative methods, such as the use of historical sales data or current data from test markets. _____ may be used in making pricing decisions, in assessing future capacity requirements, or in making decisions on whether to enter a new market.
   a. Profitability index
   b. 1990 Clean Air Act
   c. Demand forecasting
   d. 28-hour day

4. _____ is the process of estimation in unknown situations. Prediction is a similar, but more general term. Both can refer to estimation of time series, cross-sectional or longitudinal data.
   a. Forecasting
   b. 28-hour day
   c. 1990 Clean Air Act
   d. 33 Strategies of War

5. _____ is an advertisement in which a particular product specifically mentions a competitor by name for the express purpose of showing why the competitor is inferior to the product naming it.

This should not be confused with parody advertisements, where a fictional product is being advertised for the purpose of poking fun at the particular advertisement, nor should it be confused with the use of a coined brand name for the purpose of comparing the product without actually naming an actual competitor. ('Wikipedia tastes better and is less filling than the Encyclopedia Galactica.')

Chapter 4. Demand Management and Forecasting

In the 1980s, during what has been referred to as the cola wars, soft-drink manufacturer Pepsi ran a series of advertisements where people, caught on hidden camera, in a blind taste test, chose Pepsi over rival Coca-Cola.

a. 33 Strategies of War
b. 1990 Clean Air Act
c. Comparative advertising
d. 28-hour day

6. In economics, _____ is the total demand for final goods and services in the economy (Y) at a given time and price level. It is the amount of goods and services in the economy that will be purchased at all possible price levels. This is the demand for the gross domestic product of a country when inventory levels are static.
   a. A4e
   b. AAAI
   c. A Stake in the Outcome
   d. Aggregate demand

7. A _____ is the period of time between the initiation of any process of production and the completion of that process. Thus the _____ for ordering a new car from a manufacturer may be anywhere from 2 weeks to 6 months. In industry, _____ reduction is an important part of lean manufacturing.
   a. 33 Strategies of War
   b. 1990 Clean Air Act
   c. 28-hour day
   d. Lead time

8. The _____ is the amount of time an organization will look into the future when preparing a strategic plan. Many commercial companies use a five-year _____, but other organizations such as the Forestry Commission in the UK have to use a much longer _____ to form effective plans.
   a. No-bid contract
   b. Planning horizon
   c. Psychological pricing
   d. Strategic Alliance

9. A _____ is a process in which a potential employee is evaluated by an employer for prospective employment in their company, organization and was established in the late 16th century.

Chapter 4. Demand Management and Forecasting

A _____ typically precedes the hiring decision, and is used to evaluate the candidate. The interview is usually preceded by the evaluation of submitted résumés from interested candidates, then selecting a small number of candidates for interviews.

a. Supported employment
b. Payrolling
c. Split shift
d. Job interview

10. In statistics, a _____ is the difference between the actual or real and the predicted or forecast value of a time series or any other phenomenon of interest.

In simple cases, a forecast is compared with an outcome at a single time-point and a summary of _____s is constructed over a collection of such time-points. Here the forecast may be assessed using the difference or using a proportional error.

a. 33 Strategies of War
b. 28-hour day
c. 1990 Clean Air Act
d. Forecast error

11. _____ is an integrated communications-based process through which individuals and communities discover that existing and newly-identified needs and wants may be satisfied by the products and services of others.

_____ is defined by the American _____ Association as the activity, set of institutions, and processes for creating, communicating, delivering, and exchanging offerings that have value for customers, clients, partners, and society at large. The term developed from the original meaning which referred literally to going to market, as in shopping, or going to a market to buy or sell goods or services.

a. Disruptive technology
b. Market development
c. Marketing
d. Customer relationship management

Chapter 4. Demand Management and Forecasting 27

12. In statistics, _____ is:

- the arithmetic _____
- the expected value of a random variable, which is also called the population _____.

It is sometimes stated that the '_____' _____s average. This is incorrect if '_____' is taken in the specific sense of 'arithmetic _____' as there are different types of averages: the _____, median, and mode. Other simple statistical analyses use measures of spread, such as range, interquartile range, or standard deviation. For a real-valued random variable X, the _____ is the expectation of X. Note that not every probability distribution has a defined _____; see the Cauchy distribution for an example.

a. Control chart
b. Correlation
c. Statistical inference
d. Mean

13. The _____ or simply average deviation of a data set is the average of the absolute deviations and is a summary statistic of statistical dispersion or variability. It is also called the mean absolute deviation, but this is easily confused with the median absolute deviation.

The average absolute deviation of a set $\{x_1, x_2, ..., x_n\}$ is

The choice of measure of central tendency, m(X), has a marked effect on the value of the average deviation.

a. A4e
b. A Stake in the Outcome
c. AAAI
d. Average absolute deviation,

14. In statistics, signal processing, and many other fields, a _____ is a sequence of data points, measured typically at successive times, spaced at (often uniform) time intervals. _____ analysis comprises methods that attempt to understand such _____, often either to understand the underlying context of the data points (Where did they come from? What generated them?), or to make forecasts (predictions.) _____ forecasting is the use of a model to forecast future events based on known past events: to forecast future data points before they are measured.

a. Standard deviation
b. Histogram
c. Moving average
d. Time series

15. The term '_____' refers to the concept of collecting information and attempting to spot a pattern in the information. In some fields of study, the term '_____' has more formally-defined meanings.

In project management _____ is a mathematical technique that uses historical results to predict future outcome.

a. Trend analysis
b. Stepwise regression
c. Least squares
d. Regression analysis

16. In statistics, a _____ rolling mean or running average, is a type of finite impulse response filter used to analyze a set of data points by creating a series of averages of different subsets of the full data set. A _____ is not a single number, but it is a set of numbers, each of which is the average of the corresponding subset of a larger set of data points. A _____ may also use unequal weights for each data value in the subset to emphasize particular values in the subset.
a. Standard deviation
b. Time series analysis
c. Moving average
d. Homoscedastic

17. In statistics and image processing, to smooth a data set is to create an approximating function that attempts to capture important patterns in the data, while leaving out noise or other fine-scale structures/rapid phenomena. Many different algorithms are used in _____. One of the most common algorithms is the 'moving average', often used to try to capture important trends in repeated statistical surveys.
a. 1990 Clean Air Act
b. 33 Strategies of War
c. Smoothing
d. 28-hour day

18. In statistics, _____ is a technique that can be applied to time series data, either to produce smoothed data for presentation, or to make forecasts. The time series data themselves are a sequence of observations. The observed phenomenon may be an essentially random process, or it may be an orderly, but noisy, process.

Chapter 4. Demand Management and Forecasting

a. AAAI
b. A4e
c. Exponential smoothing
d. A Stake in the Outcome

19. In economics, _____s are key economic variables that economists used to predict a new phase of the business cycle. A _____ is one that changes before the economy does; a lagging indicator is one that changes after the economy has changed. Examples of _____s include stock prices, which often improve or worsen before a similar change in the economy.
   a. Perfect competition
   b. Leading indicator
   c. Deflation
   d. Human capital

20. In statistics, _____ indicates the strength and direction of a linear relationship between two random variables. That is in contrast with the usage of the term in colloquial speech, which denotes any relationship, not necessarily linear. In general statistical usage, _____ or co-relation refers to the departure of two random variables from independence.
   a. Median
   b. Time series analysis
   c. Heteroskedastic
   d. Correlation

21. The method of _____ is used to approximately solve overdetermined systems, i.e. systems of equations in which there are more equations than unknowns. _____ is often applied in statistical contexts, particularly regression analysis.

   _____ can be interpreted as a method of fitting data.

   a. Regression analysis
   b. Trend analysis
   c. Stepwise regression
   d. Least squares

Chapter 5. Capacity Planning and Master Scheduling

1. _____ is an advertisement in which a particular product specifically mentions a competitor by name for the express purpose of showing why the competitor is inferior to the product naming it.

This should not be confused with parody advertisements, where a fictional product is being advertised for the purpose of poking fun at the particular advertisement, nor should it be confused with the use of a coined brand name for the purpose of comparing the product without actually naming an actual competitor. ('Wikipedia tastes better and is less filling than the Encyclopedia Galactica.')

In the 1980s, during what has been referred to as the cola wars, soft-drink manufacturer Pepsi ran a series of advertisements where people, caught on hidden camera, in a blind taste test, chose Pepsi over rival Coca-Cola.

   a. 28-hour day
   b. 33 Strategies of War
   c. 1990 Clean Air Act
   d. Comparative advertising

2. A _____ is a plan for production, staffing, inventory, etc. It is usually linked to manufacturing where the plan indicates when and how much of each product will be demanded. This plan quantifies significant processes, parts, and other resources in order to optimize production, to identify bottlenecks, and to anticipate needs and completed goods.
   a. Remanufacturing
   b. Piecework
   c. Value engineering
   d. Master production schedule

3. _____ is the process of determining the production capacity needed by an organization to meet changing demands for its products. In the context of _____, 'capacity' is the maximum amount of work that an organization is capable of completing in a given period of time.

A discrepancy between the capacity of an organization and the demands of its customers results in inefficiency, either in under-utilized resources or unfulfilled customers.

   a. Capacity planning
   b. Remanufacturing
   c. Scientific management
   d. Productivity

4. A _____ is a group of employees from various functional areas of the organization - research, engineering, marketing, finance. human resources, and operations, for example - who are all focused on a specific objective and are responsible to work as a team to improve coordination and innovation across divisions and resolve mutual problems.

Chapter 5. Capacity Planning and Master Scheduling

a. Cross-functional team
b. Goal-setting theory
c. Graduate recruitment
d. Sociotechnical systems

5. _____ is an inventory strategy that strives to improve the return on investment of a business by reducing in-process inventory and its associated carrying costs. To meet _____ objectives, the process relies on signals between different points in the process. This means the process is often driven by a series of signals, or Kanban , which tell production when to make the next part. Kanban are usually 'tickets' but can be simple visual signals, such as the presence or absence of a part on a shelf. Implemented correctly, _____ can dramatically improve a manufacturing organization's return on investment, quality, and efficiency.

a. 1990 Clean Air Act
b. 33 Strategies of War
c. 28-hour day
d. Just-in-time

6. _____, also known as Merck Sharp ' Dohme or MSD outside the USA and Canada, is one of the largest pharmaceutical companies in the world. The headquarters of the company is located in Whitehouse Station, New Jersey, an unincorporated area in Readington Township.

a. Goodrich Corporation
b. Quest Diagnostics
c. Merck ' Co., Inc.
d. National Whistleblower Center

7. A _____ is typically described as a deliberate plan of action to guide decisions and achieve rational outcome(s.) However, the term may also be used to denote what is actually done, even though it is unplanned.

The term may apply to government, private sector organizations and groups, and individuals.

a. 1990 Clean Air Act
b. 33 Strategies of War
c. Policy
d. 28-hour day

8. In queueing theory, _____ is the proportion of the system's resources which is used by the traffic which arrives at it. It should be strictly less than one for the system to function well. It is usually represented by the symbol ρ.

a. A Stake in the Outcome
b. A4e
c. AAAI
d. Utilization

9. A _____ is the period of time between the initiation of any process of production and the completion of that process. Thus the _____ for ordering a new car from a manufacturer may be anywhere from 2 weeks to 6 months. In industry, _____ reduction is an important part of lean manufacturing.
a. 28-hour day
b. 1990 Clean Air Act
c. 33 Strategies of War
d. Lead time

10. _____ is a business function that provides a response to customer order enquiries, based on resource availability. It generates available quantities of the requested product, and delivery due dates. Therefore, _____ supports order promising and fulfillment, aiming to manage demand and match it to production plans.
a. A4e
b. A Stake in the Outcome
c. AAAI
d. Available-to-promise

Chapter 6. Order Fulfillment and Purchasing

1. _____, commonly known as e-commerce, consists of the buying and selling of products or services over electronic systems such as the Internet and other computer networks. The amount of trade conducted electronically has grown extraordinarily with widespread Internet usage. The use of commerce is conducted in this way, spurring and drawing on innovations in electronic funds transfer, supply chain management, Internet marketing, online transaction processing, electronic data interchange (EDI), inventory management systems, and automated data collection systems.

   a. Electronic Commerce
   b. Online shopping
   c. A Stake in the Outcome
   d. A4e

2. A _____ is the system of organizations, people, technology, activities, information and resources involved in moving a product or service from supplier to customer. _____ activities transform natural resources, raw materials and components into a finished product that is delivered to the end customer. In sophisticated _____ systems, used products may re-enter the _____ at any point where residual value is recyclable.

   a. Drop shipping
   b. Supply chain
   c. Wholesalers
   d. Packaging

3. _____ is the management of a network of interconnected businesses involved in the ultimate provision of product and service packages required by end customers (Harland, 1996.) _____ spans all movement and storage of raw materials, work-in-process inventory, and finished goods from point of origin to point of consumption (supply chain.)

   The definition an American professional association put forward is that _____ encompasses the planning and management of all activities involved in sourcing, procurement, conversion, and logistics management activities.

   a. Drop shipping
   b. Packaging
   c. Supply chain management
   d. Freight forwarder

4. _____ is subcontracting a process, such as product design or manufacturing, to a third-party company. The decision to outsource is often made in the interest of lowering cost or making better use of time and energy costs, redirecting or conserving energy directed at the competencies of a particular business, or to make more efficient use of land, labor, capital, (information) technology and resources. _____ became part of the business lexicon during the 1980s.

Chapter 6. Order Fulfillment and Purchasing

  a. Opinion leadership
  b. Operant conditioning
  c. Unemployment insurance
  d. Outsourcing

5. _____ is a concept related to lean and just-in-time (JIT) production. The Japanese word _____ is a common term meaning 'signboard' or 'billboard'. According to Taiichi Ohno, the man credited with developing JIT, _____ is a means through which JIT is achieved.
  a. Trademark
  b. Risk management
  c. Kanban
  d. Succession planning

6. _____ is a business term used to define an inventory categorization technique often used in materials management.

_____ provides a mechanism for identifying items which will have a significant impact on overall inventory cost whilst also providing a mechanism for identifying different categories of stock that will require different management and controls

When carrying out an _____, inventory items are valued (item cost multiplied by quantity issued/consumed in period) with the results then ranked. The results are then grouped typically into three bands.

  a. A4e
  b. AAAI
  c. A Stake in the Outcome
  d. ABC analysis

7. In economics, and cost accounting, _____ describes the total economic cost of production and is made up of variable costs, which vary according to the quantity of a good produced and include inputs such as labor and raw materials, plus fixed costs, which are independent of the quantity of a good produced and include inputs (capital) that cannot be varied in the short term, such as buildings and machinery. _____ in economics includes the total opportunity cost of each factor of production in addition to fixed and variable costs.

The rate at which _____ changes as the amount produced changes is called marginal cost.

a. 1990 Clean Air Act
b. Total cost
c. 33 Strategies of War
d. 28-hour day

8. In economics, business, retail, and accounting, a _____ is the value of money that has been used up to produce something, and hence is not available for use anymore. In economics, a _____ is an alternative that is given up as a result of a decision. In business, the _____ may be one of acquisition, in which case the amount of money expended to acquire it is counted as _____.
   a. Cost allocation
   b. Fixed costs
   c. Cost overrun
   d. Cost

9. A _____ is a type of business entity in which partners (owners) share with each other the profits or losses of the business. _____s are often favored over corporations for taxation purposes, as the _____ structure does not generally incur a tax on profits before it is distributed to the partners (i.e. there is no dividend tax levied.) However, depending on the _____ structure and the jurisdiction in which it operates, owners of a _____ may be exposed to greater personal liability than they would as shareholders of a corporation.
   a. Partnership
   b. Mediation
   c. Due process
   d. Federal Employers Liability Act

10. _____ is the management of purchasing process, and related aspects in an organization. Because of production companies purchase nowadays about 70% of their turnover, and service companies purchase approximately 40% of their turnover , _____ is one of the most critical areas in the entire organization and needs intensive management.

Purchasing Process includes as usual 8 main stages as follows:

1. Requisitioning
2. Approving
3. Studying Market
4. Making Purchase Decision
5. Placing Orders
6. Receipting Goods and Services Received
7. Accounting Goods and Services
8. Receiving Invoices and Making Payment
9. Debit note in case of material defect

_____ Process consists usually of 3 stages:

1. Purchasing Planning
2. Purchasing Tracking
3. Purchasing Reporting

Purchasing Planning may include steps as follows:

- creating purchasing projects and tasks
- providing related information (files, links, notes etc.)
- assigning purchasing tasks to employees
- setting task priorities, start/finish dates etc.
- assigning supervisors
- setting reminders

Purchasing Tracking consists of:

- checking task's status and/or history of changes
- receiving status notifications
- sorting, grouping or filtering tasks by current status
- highlighting overdue tasks

Purchasing Reporting includes:

- comparing actual and estimated values
- calculating purchasing task and project statistics
- sorting, grouping or filtering tasks by attributes
- creating charts to visualize key statistics and KPIs

a. Purchasing Management
b. Getting Things Done
c. Catfish effect
d. Cross ownership

11. _____ is one of the managerial functions like planning, organizing, staffing and directing. It is an important function because it helps to check the errors and to take the corrective action so that deviation from standards are minimized and stated goals of the organization are achieved in desired manner. According to modern concepts, _____ is a foreseeing action whereas earlier concept of _____ was used only when errors were detected. _____ in management means setting standards, measuring actual performance and taking corrective action.

Chapter 6. Order Fulfillment and Purchasing

a. Turnover
b. Decision tree pruning
c. Schedule of reinforcement
d. Control

12. _____ is a file or account that contains money that a person or company owes to suppliers, but has not paid yet (a form of debt.) When you receive an invoice you add it to the file, and then you remove it when you pay. Thus, the A/P is a form of credit that suppliers offer to their purchasers by allowing them to pay for a product or service after it has already been received.
    a. A Stake in the Outcome
    b. Accounts receivable
    c. Other revenue
    d. Accounts payable

13. In business, the term word _____ refers to a number of procurement practices, aimed at finding, evaluating and engaging suppliers of goods and services:

    - Global _____, a procurement strategy aimed at exploiting global efficiencies in production
    - Strategic _____, a component of supply chain management, for improving and re-evaluating purchasing activities
    - _____, the identification of job candidates through proactive recruiting technique
    - Co-_____, a type of auditing service
    - Low-cost country _____, a procurement strategy for acquiring materials from countries with lower labour and production costs in order to cut operating expenses
    - Corporate _____, a supply chain, purchasing/procurement, and inventory function
    - Second-tier _____, a practice of rewarding suppliers for attempting to achieve minority-owned business spending goals of their customer
    - Netsourcing, a practice of utilizing an established group of businesses, individuals, or hardware ' software applications to streamline or initiate procurement practices by tapping in to and working through a third party provider
    - Inverted _____, a price volatility reduction strategy usually conducted by procurement or supply-chain person by which the value of an organization's waste-stream is maximized by actively seeking out the highest price possible from a range of potential buyers exploiting price trends and other market factors
    - Multisourcing, a strategy that treats a given function, such as IT, as a portfolio of activities, some of which should be outsourced and others of which should be performed by internal staff.
    - Crowdsourcing, using an undefined, generally large group of people or community in the form of an open call to perform a task

In journalism, it can also refer to:

- Journalism _____, the practice of identifying a person or publication that gives information
- Single _____, the reuse of content in publishing

Chapter 6. Order Fulfillment and Purchasing

In computing, it can refer to:

- Open-_____, the act of releasing previously proprietary software under an open source/free software license
- Power _____ equipment, network devices that will provide power in a Power over Ethernet (PoE) setup

a. Reinforcement
b. Continuous
c. Cost Management
d. Sourcing

14. _____ is an inventory strategy that strives to improve the return on investment of a business by reducing in-process inventory and its associated carrying costs. To meet _____ objectives, the process relies on signals between different points in the process. This means the process is often driven by a series of signals, or Kanban , which tell production when to make the next part. Kanban are usually 'tickets' but can be simple visual signals, such as the presence or absence of a part on a shelf. Implemented correctly, _____ can dramatically improve a manufacturing organization's return on investment, quality, and efficiency.

a. 33 Strategies of War
b. Just-in-time
c. 1990 Clean Air Act
d. 28-hour day

15. The _____ is given by the United States National Institute of Standards and Technology. Through the actions of the National Productivity Advisory Committee chaired by Jack Grayson, it was established by the Malcolm Baldrige National Quality Improvement Act of 1987 - Public Law 100-107 and named for Malcolm Baldrige, who served as United States Secretary of Commerce during the Reagan administration from 1981 until his 1987 death in a rodeo accident. APQC, , organized the first White House Conference on Productivity, spearheading the creation and design of the _____ in 1987, and jointly administering the award for its first three years.

a. Scenario planning
b. Time and attendance
c. Business Network Transformation
d. Malcolm Baldrige National Quality Award

16. _____ refers to the structured transmission of data between organizations by electronic means. It is used to transfer electronic documents from one computer system to another (ie) from one trading partner to another trading partner. It is more than mere E-mail; for instance, organizations might replace bills of lading and even checks with appropriate _____ messages.

Chapter 6. Order Fulfillment and Purchasing

a. AAAI
b. A Stake in the Outcome
c. Electronic data interchange
d. A4e

17. _____ is something that a firm can do well and that meets the following three conditions:

Competencies are things that companys execute well across several business units or product sectors.

Firms usually have few competencies, but these are usually less liable to change rapidly.

1. It provides consumer benefits
2. It is not easy for competitors to imitate
3. It can be leveraged widely to many products and markets.

A _____ can take various forms, including technical/subject matter know-how, a reliable process and/or close relationships with customers and suppliers (Mascarenhas et al. 1998.)

a. Learning-by-doing
b. Dominant Design
c. NAIRU
d. Core competency

18. In microeconomics and management, the term _____ describes a style of management control. Vertically integrated companies are united through a hierarchy with a common owner. Usually each member of the hierarchy produces a different product or (market-specific) service, and the products combine to satisfy a common need.
a. 1990 Clean Air Act
b. Vertical integration
c. 33 Strategies of War
d. 28-hour day

19. _____ or Postponement is a concept in supply chain management where the manufacturing process starts by making a generic or family product that is later differentiated into a specific end-product. This is a widely used method, especially in industries with high demand uncertainty, and can be effectively used to address the final demand even if forecasts cannot be improved.

An example would be Benetton and their knitted sweaters that are initially all white, and then dyed into different colors only when the season/customer color preference/demand is known.

a. Delayed differentiation
b. Materials management
c. Supply-Chain Operations Reference
d. Demand chain

20. _____ is an advertisement in which a particular product specifically mentions a competitor by name for the express purpose of showing why the competitor is inferior to the product naming it.

This should not be confused with parody advertisements, where a fictional product is being advertised for the purpose of poking fun at the particular advertisement, nor should it be confused with the use of a coined brand name for the purpose of comparing the product without actually naming an actual competitor. ('Wikipedia tastes better and is less filling than the Encyclopedia Galactica.')

In the 1980s, during what has been referred to as the cola wars, soft-drink manufacturer Pepsi ran a series of advertisements where people, caught on hidden camera, in a blind taste test, chose Pepsi over rival Coca-Cola.

a. 1990 Clean Air Act
b. 28-hour day
c. 33 Strategies of War
d. Comparative advertising

21. _____ are a set of documents that describe an organization's policies for operation and the procedures necessary to fulfill the policies. They are often initiated because of some external requirement, such as environmental compliance or other governmental regulations, such as the American Sarbanes-Oxley Act requiring full openness in accounting practices. The easiest way to start writing _____ is to interview the users of the _____ and create a flow chart or task map or work flow of the process from start to finish.

a. Customer retention
b. Horizontal integration
c. Group booking
d. Policies and procedures

22. The '_____ scheme' is an economic term, referring to the use of commodity storage for economic stabilization. Specifically, commodities are bought and stored when there is a surplus in the economy and they are sold from these stores when there are shortages in the economy. The institutional buying, storing and selling of commodities by a large player (e.g. a government) can take place for one commodity or a 'basket of commodities'.

a. Power
b. Reservation wage
c. Contingent employment
d. Buffer stock

23. A _____ is a commercial document issued by a buyer to a seller, indicating types, quantities, and agreed prices for products or services the seller will provide to the buyer. Sending a _____ to a supplier constitutes a legal offer to buy products or services. Acceptance of a _____ by a seller usually forms a one-off contract between the buyer and seller, so no contract exists until the _____ is accepted.
   a. 33 Strategies of War
   b. Purchase order
   c. 1990 Clean Air Act
   d. 28-hour day

24. _____ is a term used by inventory specialists to describe a level of extra stock that is maintained below the cycle stock to buffer against stockouts. _____ exists to counter uncertainties in supply and demand. _____ is defined as extra units of inventory carried as protection against possible stockouts .(shortfall in raw material or packaging.)
   a. Process automation
   b. Product life cycle
   c. Knowledge worker
   d. Safety stock

25.

_____ is a systematic method to improve the 'value' of goods or products and services by using an examination of function. Value, as defined, is the ratio of function to cost. Value can therefore be increased by either improving the function or reducing the cost.

   a. Capacity planning
   b. Cellular manufacturing
   c. Master production schedule
   d. Value engineering

Chapter 7. Designing for Customers' Needs

1. A _____ is the system of organizations, people, technology, activities, information and resources involved in moving a product or service from supplier to customer. _____ activities transform natural resources, raw materials and components into a finished product that is delivered to the end customer. In sophisticated _____ systems, used products may re-enter the _____ at any point where residual value is recyclable.
   a. Packaging
   b. Wholesalers
   c. Drop shipping
   d. Supply chain

2. _____ is the management of a network of interconnected businesses involved in the ultimate provision of product and service packages required by end customers (Harland, 1996.) _____ spans all movement and storage of raw materials, work-in-process inventory, and finished goods from point of origin to point of consumption (supply chain.)

   The definition an American professional association put forward is that _____ encompasses the planning and management of all activities involved in sourcing, procurement, conversion, and logistics management activities.

   a. Freight forwarder
   b. Supply chain management
   c. Packaging
   d. Drop shipping

3. The phrase _____, according to the Organization for Economic Co-operation and Development, refers to 'creative work undertaken on a systematic basis in order to increase the stock of knowledge, including knowledge of man, culture and society, and the use of this stock of knowledge to devise new applications [sic]'

   New product design and development is more than often a crucial factor in the survival of a company. In an industry that is fast changing, firms must continually revise their design and range of products. This is necessary due to continuous technology change and development as well as other competitors and the changing preference of customers.

   a. 1990 Clean Air Act
   b. 28-hour day
   c. 33 Strategies of War
   d. Research and development

4. In economics, business, retail, and accounting, a _____ is the value of money that has been used up to produce something, and hence is not available for use anymore. In economics, a _____ is an alternative that is given up as a result of a decision. In business, the _____ may be one of acquisition, in which case the amount of money expended to acquire it is counted as _____.

a. Cost allocation
b. Cost overrun
c. Fixed costs
d. Cost

5. In probability theory, a probability distribution is called _____ if its cumulative distribution function is _____. This is equivalent to saying that for random variables X with the distribution in question, Pr[X = a] = 0 for all real numbers a, i.e.: the probability that X attains the value a is zero, for any number a. If the distribution of X is _____ then X is called a _____ random variable.

   a. Connectionist expert systems
   b. Continuous
   c. Pay Band
   d. Decision tree pruning

6. _____ is a management process whereby delivery (customer valued) processes are constantly evaluated and improved in the light of their efficiency, effectiveness and flexibility.

Some see it as a meta process for most management systems (Business Process Management, Quality Management, Project Management). Deming saw it as part of the 'system' whereby feedback from the process and customer were evaluated against organisational goals.

   a. Critical Success Factor
   b. Continuous Improvement Process
   c. Sole proprietorship
   d. First-mover advantage

7. _____ is the use of information technology to support engineers in tasks such as analysis, simulation, design, manufacture, planning, diagnosis, and repair.

Software tools that have been developed to support these activities are considered CAE tools. CAE tools are being used, for example, to analyze the robustness and performance of components and assemblies.

   a. 28-hour day
   b. 1990 Clean Air Act
   c. 33 Strategies of War
   d. Computer-aided engineering

Chapter 7. Designing for Customers' Needs

8. _____ is used for the design, development, analysis, and optimization of technical processes and is mainly applied to chemical plants and chemical processes, but also to power stations, and similar technical facilities. Process flow diagram of a typical amine treating process used in industrial plants

_____ is a model-based representation of chemical, physical, biological, and other technical processes and unit operations in software. Basic prerequisites are a thorough knowledge of chemical and physical properties of pure components and mixtures, of reactions, and of mathematical models which, in combination, allow the calculation of a process in computers.

a. 28-hour day
b. Process simulation
c. 33 Strategies of War
d. 1990 Clean Air Act

9. _____ is the process of comparing the cost, cycle time, productivity, or quality of a specific process or method to another that is widely considered to be an industry standard or best practice. Essentially, _____ provides a snapshot of the performance of your business and helps you understand where you are in relation to a particular standard. The result is often a business case for making changes in order to make improvements.

a. Complementors
b. Cost leadership
c. Competitive heterogeneity
d. Benchmarking

10. _____ is the process of discovering the technological principles of a device, object or system through analysis of its structure, function and operation. It often involves taking something (e.g., a mechanical device, electronic component, or software program) apart and analyzing its workings in detail to be used in maintenance, or to try to make a new device or program that does the same thing without copying anything from the original.

_____ has its origins in the analysis of hardware for commercial or military advantage .

a. 28-hour day
b. Predictive maintenance
c. 1990 Clean Air Act
d. Reverse engineering

11. _____ is a business management strategy aimed at embedding awareness of quality in all organizational processes. _____ has been widely used in manufacturing, education, hospitals, call centers, government, and service industries, as well as NASA space and science programs.

As defined by the International Organization for Standardization (ISO):

'_____ is a management approach for an organization, centered on quality, based on the participation of all its members and aiming at long-term success through customer satisfaction, and benefits to all members of the organization and to society.' ISO 8402:1994

One major aim is to reduce variation from every process so that greater consistency of effort is obtained. (Royse, D., Thyer, B., Padgett D., ' Logan T., 2006)

  a. Quality management
  b. 1990 Clean Air Act
  c. Total quality management
  d. 28-hour day

12. _____ is a relatively new paradigm that emerged from 'barrier-free' or 'accessible design' and 'assistive technology.' _____ strives to be a broad-spectrum solution that produces buildings, products and environments that are usable and effective for everyone, not just people with disabilities. Moreover, it recognizes the importance of how things look. For example, while built up handles are a way to make utensils more usable for people with gripping limitations, some companies introduced larger, easy to grip and attractive handles as feature of mass produced utensils.
  a. A4e
  b. A Stake in the Outcome
  c. AAAI
  d. Universal design

13. _____ is a graphic tool for defining the relationship between customer desires and the firm/product capabilities. It is a part of the Quality Function Deployment (QFD) and it utilizes a planning matrix to relate what the customer wants to how a firm (that produce the products) is going to meet those wants. It looks like a House with correlation matrix as its roof, customer wants versus product features as the main part, competitor evaluation as the porch etc.
  a. Health management system
  b. Consensus-seeking decision-making
  c. Decision Matrix
  d. House of quality

14. _____ is a 'method to transform user demands into design quality, to deploy the functions forming quality, and to deploy methods for achieving the design quality into subsystems and component parts, and ultimately to specific elements of the manufacturing process.' , as described by Dr. Yoji Akao, who originally developed _____ in Japan in 1966, when the author combined his work in quality assurance and quality control points with function deployment used in Value Engineering.

Chapter 7. Designing for Customers' Needs

_____ is designed to help planners focus on characteristics of a new or existing product or service from the viewpoints of market segments, company, or technology-development needs. The technique yields graphs and matrices.

a. Hoshin Kanri
b. Learning organization
c. 1990 Clean Air Act
d. Quality function deployment

15. _____ is the use of control systems (such as numerical control, programmable logic control, and other industrial control systems), in concert with other applications of information technology (such as computer-aided technologies [CAD, CAM, CAx]), to control industrial machinery and processes, reducing the need for human intervention. In the scope of industrialization, _____ is a step beyond mechanization. Whereas mechanization provided human operators with machinery to assist them with the physical requirements of work, _____ greatly reduces the need for human sensory and mental requirements as well.

a. Automation
b. A4e
c. AAAI
d. A Stake in the Outcome

16. The _____ is a graphical depiction of loss developed by the Japanese business statistician Genichi Taguchi to describe a phenomenon affecting the value of products produced by a company. Praised by Dr. W. Edwards Deming, it made clear the concept that quality does not suddenly plummet when, for instance, a machinist exceeds a rigid blueprint tolerance. Instead 'loss' in value progressively increases as variation increases from the intended condition. This was considered a breakthrough in describing quality, and helped fuel the continuous improvement movement that since has become known as lean manufacturing.

a. 1990 Clean Air Act
b. 33 Strategies of War
c. 28-hour day
d. Taguchi loss function

17. _____ is a pricing method used by firms. It is defined as 'a cost management tool for reducing the overall cost of a product over its entire life-cycle with the help of production, engineering, research and design'. A target cost is the maximum amount of cost that can be incurred on a product and with it the firm can still earn the required profit margin from that product at a particular selling price.

Chapter 7. Designing for Customers' Needs

a. Price war
b. Pricing objectives
c. Target costing
d. Pricing

18. In statistics, decision theory and economics, a _____ is a function that maps an event (technically an element of a sample space) onto a real number representing the economic cost or regret associated with the event.

Less technically, in statistics a _____ represents the loss (cost in money or loss in utility in some other sense) associated with an estimate being 'wrong' (different from either a desired or a true value) as a function of a measure of the degree of wrongness (generally the difference between the estimated value and the true or desired value.)

Both Frequentist and Bayesian statistical theory involve calculating statistics in such a way as to minimize the expected loss observed from being wrong given a set of assumptions about the data and one's _____.

a. 28-hour day
b. Loss function
c. 1990 Clean Air Act
d. 33 Strategies of War

19. The _____ is a measurable property of a process to the specification, expressed as a _____ index (e.g., C_{pk} or C_{pm}) or as a process performance index (e.g., P_{pk} or P_{pm}.) The output of this measurement is usually illustrated by a histogram and calculations that predict how many parts will be produced out of specification.

_____ is also defined as the capability of a process to meet its purpose as managed by an organization's management and process definition structures ISO 15504.

a. Process capability
b. Statistical process control
c. Quality control
d. Single Minute Exchange of Die

20. _____ in its literal sense is the process of transformation of local or regional phenomena into global ones. It can be described as a process by which the people of the world are unified into a single society and function together.

This process is a combination of economic, technological, sociocultural and political forces.

a. Histogram
b. Globalization
c. Collaborative Planning, Forecasting and Replenishment
d. Cost Management

21. In systems engineering, _____ is an approach that subdivides a system into smaller parts (modules) that can be independently created and then used in different systems to drive multiple functionalities. Besides reduction in cost (due to lesser customization, and less learning time), and flexibility in design, modularity offers other benefits such as augmentation (adding new solution by merely plugging in a new module), and exclusion. Examples of modular systems are cars, computers and high rise buildings.
   a. 28-hour day
   b. 1990 Clean Air Act
   c. Statement of work
   d. Modular design

22. A _____ is a computer program typically used to provide some form of artificial intelligence, which consists primarily of a set of rules about behavior. These rules, termed productions, are a basic representation found useful in AI planning, expert systems and action selection. A _____ provides the mechanism necessary to execute productions in order to achieve some goal for the system.
   a. 28-hour day
   b. 1990 Clean Air Act
   c. 33 Strategies of War
   d. Production system

23. _____ is the frequency with which an engineered system or component fails, expressed for example in failures per hour. It is often denoted by the Greek letter >λ and is important in reliability theory.

The _____ of a system usually depends on time, with the rate varying over the life cycle of the system.

   a. Failure rate
   b. Heteroskedastic
   c. Correlation
   d. Statistics

Chapter 7. Designing for Customers' Needs 49

24. In statistics, _____ is:

- the arithmetic _____
- the expected value of a random variable, which is also called the population _____.

It is sometimes stated that the '_____' _____s average. This is incorrect if '_____' is taken in the specific sense of 'arithmetic _____' as there are different types of averages: the _____, median, and mode. Other simple statistical analyses use measures of spread, such as range, interquartile range, or standard deviation. For a real-valued random variable X, the _____ is the expectation of X. Note that not every probability distribution has a defined _____; see the Cauchy distribution for an example.

a. Statistical inference
b. Correlation
c. Control chart
d. Mean

25. _____ is the arithmetic mean (average) time between failures of a system. The _____ is typically part of a model that assumes the failed system is immediately repaired (zero elapsed time), as a part of a renewal process. This is in contrast to the mean time to failure (MTTF), which measures average time between failure with the modeling assumption that the failed system is not repaired.

a. Mean time between failures
b. 1990 Clean Air Act
c. 33 Strategies of War
d. 28-hour day

26. _____ is the average time that a device will take to recover from any failure. Examples of such devices range from self-resetting fuses (where the _____ would be very short, probably seconds), up to whole systems which have to be repaired or replaced.

The _____ would usually be part of a maintenance contract, where the user would pay more for a system whose _____ was 24 hours, than for one of, say, 7 days.

a. 28-hour day
b. Mean time to recovery
c. 33 Strategies of War
d. 1990 Clean Air Act

Chapter 7. Designing for Customers' Needs

27. A _____ is a relatively new executive level position at a corporation, company, organization typically reporting directly to the CEO or board of directors. The _____ is responsible for a brand's image, experience, and promise, and propagating it throughout all aspects of the company. The brand officer oversees marketing, advertising, design, public relations and customer service departments.
   a. Chief executive officer
   b. Chief brand officer
   c. Purchasing manager
   d. Director of communications

28. The _____, widely known as ISO, is an international-standard-setting body composed of representatives from various national standards organizations. Founded on 23 February 1947, the organization promulgates worldwide proprietary industrial and commercial standards. It is headquartered in Geneva, Switzerland.
   a. A Stake in the Outcome
   b. International Organization for Standardization
   c. AAAI
   d. A4e

29. An _____ is the negative aspects of human activity on the biophysical environment. Environmentalism, a social and environmental movement that started in the 1960s, focuses on addressing _____s through advocacy, education and activism.

Major current _____s are climate change, pollution and resource depletion.

   a. AAAI
   b. Environmental issue
   c. A Stake in the Outcome
   d. A4e

30. _____ is an advertisement in which a particular product specifically mentions a competitor by name for the express purpose of showing why the competitor is inferior to the product naming it.

This should not be confused with parody advertisements, where a fictional product is being advertised for the purpose of poking fun at the particular advertisement, nor should it be confused with the use of a coined brand name for the purpose of comparing the product without actually naming an actual competitor. ('Wikipedia tastes better and is less filling than the Encyclopedia Galactica.')

In the 1980s, during what has been referred to as the cola wars, soft-drink manufacturer Pepsi ran a series of advertisements where people, caught on hidden camera, in a blind taste test, chose Pepsi over rival Coca-Cola.

a. 1990 Clean Air Act
b. Comparative advertising
c. 33 Strategies of War
d. 28-hour day

Chapter 8. The Quality Imperative

1. _____ is a business management strategy aimed at embedding awareness of quality in all organizational processes. _____ has been widely used in manufacturing, education, hospitals, call centers, government, and service industries, as well as NASA space and science programs.

As defined by the International Organization for Standardization (ISO):

'_____ is a management approach for an organization, centered on quality, based on the participation of all its members and aiming at long-term success through customer satisfaction, and benefits to all members of the organization and to society.' ISO 8402:1994

One major aim is to reduce variation from every process so that greater consistency of effort is obtained. (Royse, D., Thyer, B., Padgett D., ' Logan T., 2006)

a. Quality management
b. 28-hour day
c. 1990 Clean Air Act
d. Total quality management

2. _____ can be considered to have three main components: quality control, quality assurance and quality improvement. _____ is focused not only on product quality, but also the means to achieve it. _____ therefore uses quality assurance and control of processes as well as products to achieve more consistent quality.

a. 1990 Clean Air Act
b. Total quality management
c. 28-hour day
d. Quality management

3. _____ is an advertisement in which a particular product specifically mentions a competitor by name for the express purpose of showing why the competitor is inferior to the product naming it.

This should not be confused with parody advertisements, where a fictional product is being advertised for the purpose of poking fun at the particular advertisement, nor should it be confused with the use of a coined brand name for the purpose of comparing the product without actually naming an actual competitor. ('Wikipedia tastes better and is less filling than the Encyclopedia Galactica.')

In the 1980s, during what has been referred to as the cola wars, soft-drink manufacturer Pepsi ran a series of advertisements where people, caught on hidden camera, in a blind taste test, chose Pepsi over rival Coca-Cola.

a. 28-hour day
b. 1990 Clean Air Act
c. 33 Strategies of War
d. Comparative advertising

4. The _____ was a period in the late 18th and early 19th centuries when major changes in agriculture, manufacturing, mining, and transportation had a profound effect on the socioeconomic and cultural conditions in Britain. The changes subsequently spread throughout Europe, North America, and eventually the world. The onset of the _____ marked a major turning point in human society; almost every aspect of daily life was eventually influenced in some way.
   a. Adam Smith
   b. Affiliation
   c. Abraham Harold Maslow
   d. Industrial Revolution

5. _____ refers to planned and systematic production processes that provide confidence in a product's suitability for its intended purpose. Refer to the definition by Merriam-Webster for further information . It is a set of activities intended to ensure that products (goods and/or services) satisfy customer requirements in a systematic, reliable fashion.
   a. 28-hour day
   b. Quality assurance
   c. 1990 Clean Air Act
   d. Risk assessment

6. _____ is a broad label that refers to any individuals or households that use goods and services generated within the economy. The concept of a _____ is used in different contexts, so that the usage and significance of the term may vary.

Typically when business people and economists talk of _____s they are talking about person as _____, an aggregated commodity item with little individuality other than that expressed in the buy/not-buy decision.

   a. 1990 Clean Air Act
   b. 28-hour day
   c. Consumer
   d. 33 Strategies of War

Chapter 8. The Quality Imperative

7. The _____ was enacted in 1972 by the United States Congress. It established the United States Consumer Product Safety Commission as an independent agency of the United States federal government and defined its basic authority. The act gives CPSC the power to develop safety standards and pursue recalls for products that present unreasonable or substantial risks of injury or death to consumers.

   a. 28-hour day
   b. 1990 Clean Air Act
   c. 33 Strategies of War
   d. Consumer Product Safety Act

8. _____ is the equation of personal happiness with consumption and the purchase of material possessions. The term is often associated with criticisms of consumption starting with Thorstein Veblen or, more recently by a movement called Enoughism.

   Veblen's subject of examination, the newly emergent middle class arising at the turn of the twentieth century, comes to full fruition by the end of the twentieth century through the process of globalization.

   In economics, _____ refers to economic policies placing emphasis on consumption.

   a. Market culture
   b. 1990 Clean Air Act
   c. 28-hour day
   d. Consumerism

9. _____ is the area of law in which manufacturers, distributors, suppliers, retailers, and others who make products available to the public are held responsible for the injuries those products cause.

   In the United States, the claims most commonly associated with _____ are negligence, strict liability, breach of warranty, and various consumer protection claims. The majority of _____ laws are determined at the state level and vary widely from state to state.

   a. Leave of absence
   b. Right-to-work laws
   c. Railway Labor Act
   d. Product Liability

10. _____ is an area of business concerned with the production of goods and services, and involves the responsibility of ensuring that business operations are efficient in terms of using as little resource as needed, and effective in terms of meeting customer requirements. It is concerned with managing the process that converts inputs (in the forms of materials, labour and energy) into outputs (in the form of goods and services).

Chapter 8. The Quality Imperative

Operations traditionally refers to the production of goods and services separately, although the distinction between these two main types of operations is increasingly difficult to make as manufacturers tend to merge product and service offerings.

a. A4e
b. AAAI
c. Operations management
d. A Stake in the Outcome

11. _____ is a term defined by the Oxford English Dictionary as an individual's 'course or progress through life '. It is usually considered to pertain to remunerative work (and sometimes also formal education.)

The etymology of the term is somewhat ironic in that it comes from the Latin word carrera, which means race .

a. Nursing shortage
b. Career planning
c. Spatial mismatch
d. Career

12. In economics, business, retail, and accounting, a _____ is the value of money that has been used up to produce something, and hence is not available for use anymore. In economics, a _____ is an alternative that is given up as a result of a decision. In business, the _____ may be one of acquisition, in which case the amount of money expended to acquire it is counted as _____.

a. Fixed costs
b. Cost overrun
c. Cost allocation
d. Cost

13. Engineering _____ is the permissible limit of variation in

1. a physical dimension,
2. a measured value or physical property of a material, manufactured object, system, or service,
3. other measured values (such as temperature, humidity, etc.)
4. in engineering and safety, a physical distance or space (_____), as in a truck (lorry), train or boat under a bridge as well as a train in a tunnel

Dimensions, properties, or conditions may vary within certain practical limits without significantly affecting functioning of equipment or a process. _____s are specified to allow reasonable leeway for imperfections and inherent variability without compromising performance.

Chapter 8. The Quality Imperative

The _____ may be specified as a factor or percentage of the nominal value, a maximum deviation from a nominal value, an explicit range of allowed values, be specified by a note or published standard with this information, or be implied by the numeric accuracy of the nominal value. _____ can be symmetrical, as in 40±0.1, or asymmetrical, such as 40+0.2/−0.1.

a. Zero defects
b. Quality assurance
c. Root cause analysis
d. Tolerance

14. A _____ is the period of time between the initiation of any process of production and the completion of that process. Thus the _____ for ordering a new car from a manufacturer may be anywhere from 2 weeks to 6 months. In industry, _____ reduction is an important part of lean manufacturing.

a. 33 Strategies of War
b. Lead time
c. 1990 Clean Air Act
d. 28-hour day

15. In statistics, decision theory and economics, a _____ is a function that maps an event (technically an element of a sample space) onto a real number representing the economic cost or regret associated with the event.

Less technically, in statistics a _____ represents the loss (cost in money or loss in utility in some other sense) associated with an estimate being 'wrong' (different from either a desired or a true value) as a function of a measure of the degree of wrongness (generally the difference between the estimated value and the true or desired value.)

Both Frequentist and Bayesian statistical theory involve calculating statistics in such a way as to minimize the expected loss observed from being wrong given a set of assumptions about the data and one's _____.

a. 1990 Clean Air Act
b. 33 Strategies of War
c. Loss function
d. 28-hour day

16. The general definition of an _____ is an evaluation of a person, organization, system, process, project or product. _____s are performed to ascertain the validity and reliability of information; also to provide an assessment of a system's internal control. The goal of an _____ is to express an opinion on the person / organization/system (etc) in question, under evaluation based on work done on a test basis.

Chapter 8. The Quality Imperative 57

a. Audit committee
b. Audit
c. A Stake in the Outcome
d. Internal control

17. The _____ is given by the United States National Institute of Standards and Technology. Through the actions of the National Productivity Advisory Committee chaired by Jack Grayson, it was established by the Malcolm Baldrige National Quality Improvement Act of 1987 - Public Law 100-107 and named for Malcolm Baldrige, who served as United States Secretary of Commerce during the Reagan administration from 1981 until his 1987 death in a rodeo accident. APQC, , organized the first White House Conference on Productivity, spearheading the creation and design of the _____ in 1987, and jointly administering the award for its first three years.

a. Business Network Transformation
b. Scenario planning
c. Time and attendance
d. Malcolm Baldrige National Quality Award

18. In business, operating margin, operating income margin, operating profit margin or _____ is the ratio of operating income (operating profit in the UK) divided by net sales, usually presented in percent.

> ☒

(Relevant figures in italics)

> ☒

It is a measurement of what proportion of a company's revenue is left over, before taxes and other indirect costs (such as rent, bonus, interest, etc.), after paying for variable costs of production as wages, raw materials, etc. A good operating margin is needed for a company to be able to pay for its fixed costs, such as interest on debt.

a. P/E ratio
b. Rate of return
c. Return on sales
d. Return on equity

19. The _____ establishes relationships among profitablity, customer loyalty, and employee satisfaction, loyalty, and productivity. The links in the chain (which should be regarded as propositions) as follows: Profit and growth are stimulated primarily by customer loyalty. Loyalty is a direct result of customer satisfaction.

Chapter 8. The Quality Imperative

   a. Chief privacy officer
   b. Letter of resignation
   c. Service-profit chain
   d. Corner office

20. _____ is the process of comparing the cost, cycle time, productivity, or quality of a specific process or method to another that is widely considered to be an industry standard or best practice. Essentially, _____ provides a snapshot of the performance of your business and helps you understand where you are in relation to a particular standard. The result is often a business case for making changes in order to make improvements.
   a. Cost leadership
   b. Competitive heterogeneity
   c. Complementors
   d. Benchmarking

21. _____ refers to metrics and measures of output from production processes, per unit of input. Labor _____, for example, is typically measured as a ratio of output per labor-hour, an input. _____ may be conceived of as a metrics of the technical or engineering efficiency of production.
   a. Productivity
   b. Value engineering
   c. Remanufacturing
   d. Master production schedule

22. _____ refers to the movement of cash into or out of a business or financial product. It is usually measured during a specified, finite period of time. Measurement of _____ can be used

   - to determine a project's rate of return or value. The time of _____s into and out of projects are used as inputs in financial models such as internal rate of return, and net present value.
   - to determine problems with a business's liquidity. Being profitable does not necessarily mean being liquid. A company can fail because of a shortage of cash, even while profitable.
   - as an alternate measure of a business's profits when it is believed that accrual accounting concepts do not represent economic realities. For example, a company may be notionally profitable but generating little operational cash (as may be the case for a company that barters its products rather than selling for cash.) In such a case, the company may be deriving additional operating cash by issuing shares evaluating default risk, re-investment requirements, etc.

_____ is a generic term used differently depending on the context. It may be defined by users for their own purposes.

Chapter 8. The Quality Imperative

a. Gross profit margin
b. Gross profit
c. Sweat equity
d. Cash flow

23. _____ is the discipline of planning, organizing and managing resources to bring about the successful completion of specific project goals and objectives. It is often closely related to and sometimes conflated with Program management.

A project is a finite endeavor--having specific start and completion dates--undertaken to meet particular goals and objectives, usually to bring about beneficial change or added value.

a. Precedence diagram
b. Project engineer
c. Work package
d. Project management

24. The _____, widely known as ISO , is an international-standard-setting body composed of representatives from various national standards organizations. Founded on 23 February 1947, the organization promulgates worldwide proprietary industrial and commercial standards. It is headquartered in Geneva, Switzerland.

a. AAAI
b. A4e
c. A Stake in the Outcome
d. International Organization for Standardization

25. A _____ is a volunteer group composed of workers (or even students), usually under the leadership of their supervisor (but they can elect a team leader), who are trained to identify, analyse and solve work-related problems and present their solutions to management in order to improve the performance of the organization, and motivate and enrich the work of employees. When matured, true _____s become self-managing, having gained the confidence of management. _____s are an alternative to the dehumanising concept of the Division of Labour, where workers or individuals are treated like robots.

a. Certified in Production and Inventory Management
b. Competency-based job descriptions
c. Connectionist expert systems
d. Quality circle

26. _____ is the state or fact of exclusive rights and control over property, which may be an object, land/real estate or intellectual property. An _____ right is also referred to as title. The concept of _____ has existed for thousands of years and in all cultures.

Chapter 8. The Quality Imperative

a. Emanation of the state
b. A4e
c. Ownership
d. A Stake in the Outcome

27. _____ is one of the managerial functions like planning, organizing, staffing and directing. It is an important function because it helps to check the errors and to take the corrective action so that deviation from standards are minimized and stated goals of the organization are achieved in desired manner. According to modern concepts, _____ is a foreseeing action whereas earlier concept of _____ was used only when errors were detected. _____ in management means setting standards, measuring actual performance and taking corrective action.
   a. Decision tree pruning
   b. Turnover
   c. Schedule of reinforcement
   d. Control

28. _____ ('Plan-Do-Check-Act') is an iterative four-step problem-solving process typically used in business process improvement. It is also known as the Deming Cycle, Shewhart cycle, Deming Wheel, or Plan-Do-Study-Act.

_____ was made popular by Dr. W. Edwards Deming, who is considered by many to be the father of modern quality control; however it was always referred to by him as the Shewhart cycle. Later in Deming's career, he modified _____ to Plan, Do, Study, Act (PDSA) so as to better describe his recommendations.

   a. Decentralization
   b. Management team
   c. Management by exception
   d. PDCA

29. In engineering and manufacturing, _____ and quality engineering are used in developing systems to ensure products or services are designed and produced to meet or exceed customer requirements. Refer to the definition by Merriam-Webster for further information . These systems are often developed in conjunction with other business and engineering disciplines using a cross-functional approach.
   a. Single Minute Exchange of Die
   b. Statistical process control
   c. Quality Control
   d. Process capability

30. The concept of _____ is a means to quantify the total cost of quality-related efforts and deficiencies. It was first described by Armand V. Feigenbaum in a 1956 Harvard Business Review article.

Chapter 8. The Quality Imperative

Prior to its introduction, the general perception was that higher quality requires higher costs, either by buying better materials or machines or by hiring more labor.

a. Cost overrun
b. Transaction cost
c. Variable cost
d. Quality costs

31. In quality assessment, _____ is an inspection standard describing the maximum number of defects that could be considered acceptable during the random sampling of an inspection. The defects found during inspection are classified into three levels: critical, major and minor. Broadly, these levels are defined as follows:

- Critical defects are those that render the product unsafe or hazardous for the end user, or that contravene mandatory regulations.

- Major defects can result in the product's failure, reducing its marketability, usability, or saleability.

- Minor defects do not affect the product's marketability or usability, but represent workmanship defects that make the product fall short of defined quality standards.

Different companies maintain different interpretations of each defect type.

a. AAAI
b. A4e
c. Acceptable quality level
d. A Stake in the Outcome

32. _____ is the design of all information-gathering exercises where variation is present, whether under the full control of the experimenter or not. (The latter situation is usually called an observational study.) Often the experimenter is interested in the effect of some process or intervention (the 'treatment') on some objects (the 'experimental units'), which may be people, parts of people, groups of people, etc.

a. 28-hour day
b. 1990 Clean Air Act
c. Taguchi methods
d. Design of experiments

33. _____ testing is a systematic, statistical way of testing. _____s could be applied in user interface testing, system testing, regression testing, configuration testing and performance testing.

a. AAAI
b. A Stake in the Outcome
c. A4e
d. Orthogonal array

34. '_____' is Step 7 of 'Philip Crosby's 14 Step Quality Improvement Process'. Although applicable to any type of enterprise, it has been primarily adopted within industry supply chains wherever large volumes of components are being purchased (common items such as nuts and bolts are good examples.)

_____ was a quality control program originated by the Denver Division of the Martin Marietta Corporation (now Lockheed Martin) on the Titan Missile program, which carried the first astronauts into space in the late 1960s.

a. 28-hour day
b. Root cause analysis
c. 1990 Clean Air Act
d. Zero defects

35. A _____ is typically described as a deliberate plan of action to guide decisions and achieve rational outcome(s.) However, the term may also be used to denote what is actually done, even though it is unplanned.

The term may apply to government, private sector organizations and groups, and individuals.

a. 33 Strategies of War
b. Policy
c. 1990 Clean Air Act
d. 28-hour day

Chapter 9. Process Control and Improvement

1. _____ is one of the managerial functions like planning, organizing, staffing and directing. It is an important function because it helps to check the errors and to take the corrective action so that deviation from standards are minimized and stated goals of the organization are achieved in desired manner. According to modern concepts, _____ is a foreseeing action whereas earlier concept of _____ was used only when errors were detected. _____ in management means setting standards, measuring actual performance and taking corrective action.
   a. Decision tree pruning
   b. Schedule of reinforcement
   c. Turnover
   d. Control

2. In organizational development (OD), _____ is a series of actions taken by a Process Owner to identify, analyze and improve existing processes within an organization to meet new goals and objectives. These actions often follow a specific methodology or strategy to create successful results. A sampling of these are listed below.
   a. Product innovation
   b. Letter of resignation
   c. Process improvement
   d. Supervisory board

3. Procter is a surname, and may also refer to:

   - Bryan Waller Procter (pseud. Barry Cornwall), English poet
   - Goodwin Procter, American law firm
   - _____, consumer products multinational

   a. Procter ' Gamble
   b. Downstream
   c. Master and Servant Acts
   d. Strict liability

4. In engineering and manufacturing, _____ and quality engineering are used in developing systems to ensure products or services are designed and produced to meet or exceed customer requirements. Refer to the definition by Merriam-Webster for further information. These systems are often developed in conjunction with other business and engineering disciplines using a cross-functional approach.
   a. Process capability
   b. Single Minute Exchange of Die
   c. Quality Control
   d. Statistical process control

Chapter 9. Process Control and Improvement

5. _____ describes the situation when output from (or information about the result of) an event or phenomenon in the past will influence the same event/phenomenon in the present or future. When an event is part of a chain of cause-and-effect that forms a circuit or loop, then the event is said to 'feed back' into itself.

_____ is also a synonym for:

- _____ signal; the information about the initial event that is the basis for subsequent modification of the event.
- _____ loop; the causal path that leads from the initial generation of the _____ signal to the subsequent modification of the event.

_____ is a mechanism, process or signal that is looped back to control a system within itself. Such a loop is called a _____ loop.

a. Feedback loop
b. Feedback
c. 1990 Clean Air Act
d. Positive feedback

6. The _____ is a measurable property of a process to the specification, expressed as a _____ index (e.g., C_{pk} or C_{pm}) or as a process performance index (e.g., P_{pk} or P_{pm}.) The output of this measurement is usually illustrated by a histogram and calculations that predict how many parts will be produced out of specification.

_____ is also defined as the capability of a process to meet its purpose as managed by an organization's management and process definition structures ISO 15504.

a. Single Minute Exchange of Die
b. Statistical process control
c. Quality control
d. Process capability

Chapter 9. Process Control and Improvement

7. In quality assessment, _____ is an inspection standard describing the maximum number of defects that could be considered acceptable during the random sampling of an inspection. The defects found during inspection are classified into three levels: critical, major and minor. Broadly, these levels are defined as follows:

- Critical defects are those that render the product unsafe or hazardous for the end user, or that contravene mandatory regulations.

- Major defects can result in the product's failure, reducing its marketability, usability, or saleability.

- Minor defects do not affect the product's marketability or usability, but represent workmanship defects that make the product fall short of defined quality standards.

Different companies maintain different interpretations of each defect type.

  a. Acceptable quality level
  b. A4e
  c. A Stake in the Outcome
  d. AAAI

8. In _____, tests are carried out to the specimen's failure, in order to understand a specimen's structural performance or material behaviour under different loads. These tests are generally much easier to carry out, yield more information, and are easier to interpret than nondestructive testing.

_____ is most suitable, and economic, for objects which will be mass produced, as the cost of destroying a small number of specimens is negligible.

  a. 28-hour day
  b. Destructive testing
  c. 1990 Clean Air Act
  d. 33 Strategies of War

9. _____ is an effective method of monitoring a process through the use of control charts. Control charts enable the use of objective criteria for distinguishing background variation from events of significance based on statistical techniques. Much of its power lies in the ability to monitor both process center and its variation about that center.
  a. Single Minute Exchange of Die
  b. Quality control
  c. Process capability
  d. Statistical process control

Chapter 9. Process Control and Improvement

10. _____ is one of the four elements of marketing mix. An organization or set of organizations (go-betweens) involved in the process of making a product or service available for use or consumption by a consumer or business user.

The other three parts of the marketing mix are product, pricing, and promotion.

   a. Matching theory
   b. Job creation programs
   c. Distribution
   d. Missing completely at random

11. In statistics, _____ is:

   - the arithmetic _____
   - the expected value of a random variable, which is also called the population _____.

It is sometimes stated that the '_____' _____s average. This is incorrect if '_____' is taken in the specific sense of 'arithmetic _____' as there are different types of averages: the _____, median, and mode. Other simple statistical analyses use measures of spread, such as range, interquartile range, or standard deviation. For a real-valued random variable X, the _____ is the expectation of X. Note that not every probability distribution has a defined _____; see the Cauchy distribution for an example.

   a. Statistical inference
   b. Correlation
   c. Mean
   d. Control chart

12. _____ refers to the movement of cash into or out of a business or financial product. It is usually measured during a specified, finite period of time. Measurement of _____ can be used

   - to determine a project's rate of return or value. The time of _____s into and out of projects are used as inputs in financial models such as internal rate of return, and net present value.
   - to determine problems with a business's liquidity. Being profitable does not necessarily mean being liquid. A company can fail because of a shortage of cash, even while profitable.
   - as an alternate measure of a business's profits when it is believed that accrual accounting concepts do not represent economic realities. For example, a company may be notionally profitable but generating little operational cash (as may be the case for a company that barters its products rather than selling for cash.) In such a case, the company may be deriving additional operating cash by issuing shares evaluating default risk, re-investment requirements, etc.

_____ is a generic term used differently depending on the context. It may be defined by users for their own purposes.

Chapter 9. Process Control and Improvement

a. Gross profit
b. Sweat equity
c. Gross profit margin
d. Cash flow

13. _____ refers to bodies of techniques for investigating phenomena, acquiring new knowledge, or correcting and integrating previous knowledge. To be termed scientific, a method of inquiry must be based on gathering observable, empirical and measurable evidence subject to specific principles of reasoning. A _____ consists of the collection of data through observation and experimentation, and the formulation and testing of hypotheses.
   a. 1990 Clean Air Act
   b. 33 Strategies of War
   c. 28-hour day
   d. Scientific method

14. In statistics, a _____ is a graphical display of tabulated frequencies, shown as bars. It shows what proportion of cases fall into each of several categories: it is a form of data binning. The categories are usually specified as non-overlapping intervals of some variable.
   a. Standard deviation
   b. Correlation
   c. Histogram
   d. Statistics

15. _____ is a statistical technique in decision making that is used for selection of a limited number of tasks that produce significant overall effect. It uses the Pareto principle - the idea that by doing 20% of work you can generate 80% of the advantage of doing the entire job. Or in terms of quality improvement, a large majority of problems (80%) are produced by a few key causes (20%.)
   a. Goodness of fit
   b. Polychoric correlation
   c. Probability matching
   d. Pareto analysis

16. _____s are diagrams that show the causes of a certain event. A common use of the _____ is in product design, to identify potential factors causing an overall effect.

_____s were proposed by Kaoru Ishikawa in the 1960s, who pioneered quality management processes in the Kawasaki shipyards, and in the process became one of the founding fathers of modern management.

Chapter 9. Process Control and Improvement

a. Ishikawa diagram
b. AAAI
c. A Stake in the Outcome
d. A4e

17. _____ is the design of all information-gathering exercises where variation is present, whether under the full control of the experimenter or not. (The latter situation is usually called an observational study.) Often the experimenter is interested in the effect of some process or intervention (the 'treatment') on some objects (the 'experimental units'), which may be people, parts of people, groups of people, etc.
   a. 28-hour day
   b. Design of experiments
   c. Taguchi methods
   d. 1990 Clean Air Act

18. In statistics, _____ indicates the strength and direction of a linear relationship between two random variables. That is in contrast with the usage of the term in colloquial speech, which denotes any relationship, not necessarily linear. In general statistical usage, _____ or co-relation refers to the departure of two random variables from independence.
   a. Heteroskedastic
   b. Median
   c. Correlation
   d. Time series analysis

19. A scatter plot is a type of display using Cartesian coordinates to display values for two variables for a set of data.

The data is displayed as a collection of points, each having the value of one variable determining the position on the horizontal axis and the value of the other variable determining the position on the vertical axis. A scatter plot is also called a scatter chart, _____ and scatter graph.

   a. 33 Strategies of War
   b. 28-hour day
   c. 1990 Clean Air Act
   d. Scatter diagram

20. The _____ in statistical process control is a tool used to determine whether a manufacturing or business process is in a state of statistical control or not.

Chapter 9. Process Control and Improvement

If the chart indicates that the process is currently under control then it can be used with confidence to predict the future performance of the process. If the chart indicates that the process being monitored is not in control, the pattern it reveals can help determine the source of variation to be eliminated to bring the process back into control.

a. Failure rate
b. Simple moving average
c. Time series analysis
d. Control chart

21. In probability theory and statistics, _____ is a measure of the variability or dispersion of a population, a data set, or a probability distribution. A low _____ indicates that the data points tend to be very close to the same value (the mean), while high _____ indicates that the data are 'spread out' over a large range of values.

For example, the average height for adult men in the United States is about 70 inches (178 cm), with a _____ of around 3 in (8 cm.)

a. Normal distribution
b. Frequency distribution
c. Failure rate
d. Standard deviation

22. In process improvement efforts, the _____ or process capability ratio is a statistical measure of process capability: The ability of a process to produce output within engineering tolerances and specification limits. The concept of process capability only holds meaning for processes that are in a state of statistical control.

If the upper and lower specifications of the process are USL and LSL, the target process mean is T, the estimated mean of the process is $\hat{\mu}$ and the estimated variability of the process (expressed as a standard deviation) is $\hat{\sigma}$, then commonly-accepted process capability indices include:

$\hat{\sigma}$ is estimated using the sample standard deviation.

a. 1990 Clean Air Act
b. Process capability ratio
c. Constant dollars
d. Process capability index

Chapter 9. Process Control and Improvement

23. _____ is an advertisement in which a particular product specifically mentions a competitor by name for the express purpose of showing why the competitor is inferior to the product naming it.

This should not be confused with parody advertisements, where a fictional product is being advertised for the purpose of poking fun at the particular advertisement, nor should it be confused with the use of a coined brand name for the purpose of comparing the product without actually naming an actual competitor. ('Wikipedia tastes better and is less filling than the Encyclopedia Galactica.')

In the 1980s, during what has been referred to as the cola wars, soft-drink manufacturer Pepsi ran a series of advertisements where people, caught on hidden camera, in a blind taste test, chose Pepsi over rival Coca-Cola.

a. 33 Strategies of War
b. 28-hour day
c. 1990 Clean Air Act
d. Comparative advertising

Chapter 10. Flow-Control: Eliminating Process Waste

1. In economics, business, retail, and accounting, a _____ is the value of money that has been used up to produce something, and hence is not available for use anymore. In economics, a _____ is an alternative that is given up as a result of a decision. In business, the _____ may be one of acquisition, in which case the amount of money expended to acquire it is counted as _____.
    a. Cost overrun
    b. Fixed costs
    c. Cost allocation
    d. Cost

2. _____ is one of the managerial functions like planning, organizing, staffing and directing. It is an important function because it helps to check the errors and to take the corrective action so that deviation from standards are minimized and stated goals of the organization are achieved in desired manner. According to modern concepts, _____ is a foreseeing action whereas earlier concept of _____ was used only when errors were detected. _____ in management means setting standards, measuring actual performance and taking corrective action.
    a. Control
    b. Turnover
    c. Schedule of reinforcement
    d. Decision tree pruning

3. _____ are costs incurred on the purchase of land, buildings, construction and equipment to be used in the production of goods or the rendering of services. In other words, the total cost needed to bring a project to a commercially operable status. However, _____ are not limited to the initial construction of a factory or other business.
    a. Contingent employment
    b. Capital costs
    c. Fixed asset turnover
    d. Reservation wage

4. In business management, _____ is money spent to keep and maintain a stock of goods in storage.
The most obvious _____s include rent for the required space; equipment, materials, and labor to operate the space; insurance; security; interest on money invested in the inventory and space, and other direct expenses. Some stored goods become obsolete before they are sold, reducing their contribution to revenue while having no effect on their _____.

    a. Choquet integral
    b. Holding cost
    c. Market niche
    d. Private placement

Chapter 10. Flow-Control: Eliminating Process Waste

5. _____ is the state of being which occurs when a person, object, or service is no longer wanted even though it may still be in good working order. _____ frequently occurs because a replacement has become available that is superior in one or more aspects. Videotapes making way for DVDs

Technical _____ may occur when a new product or technology supersedes the old, and it becomes preferred to utilize the new technology in place of the old.

   a. A4e
   b. AAAI
   c. A Stake in the Outcome
   d. Obsolescence

6. _____: A distribution term that refers to the status of items on a purchase order in the event that some or all of the inventory required to fulfill the order is insufficient to satisfy demand. This differs from a forward order where stock is available but delivery is postponed for another reason.

   _____ Cost: A cost incurred by a business when it is unable to fill an order and must complete it later.

   a. Backorder
   b. Mass market
   c. Chief analytics officer
   d. Chief privacy officer

7. The _____ is given by the United States National Institute of Standards and Technology. Through the actions of the National Productivity Advisory Committee chaired by Jack Grayson, it was established by the Malcolm Baldrige National Quality Improvement Act of 1987 - Public Law 100-107 and named for Malcolm Baldrige, who served as United States Secretary of Commerce during the Reagan administration from 1981 until his 1987 death in a rodeo accident. APQC, , organized the first White House Conference on Productivity, spearheading the creation and design of the _____ in 1987, and jointly administering the award for its first three years.
   a. Scenario planning
   b. Business Network Transformation
   c. Malcolm Baldrige National Quality Award
   d. Time and attendance

8. The metastability in flip-flops can be avoided by ensuring that the data and control inputs are held valid and constant for specified periods before and after the clock pulse, called the _____ and the hold time (t_h) respectively. These times are specified in the data sheet for the device, and are typically between a few nanoseconds and a few hundred picoseconds for modern devices.

Unfortunately, it is not always possible to meet the setup and hold criteria, because the flip-flop may be connected to a real-time signal that could change at any time, outside the control of the designer.

a. 33 Strategies of War
b. Setup time
c. 1990 Clean Air Act
d. 28-hour day

9. The _____ of an edge is $c_f(u,v) = c(u,v) - f(u,v)$. This defines a residual network denoted $G_f(V, E_f)$, giving the amount of available capacity. See that there can be an edge from u to v in the residual network, even though there is no edge from u to v in the original network.

a. 28-hour day
b. 33 Strategies of War
c. 1990 Clean Air Act
d. Residual capacity

10. _____ refers to the movement of cash into or out of a business or financial product. It is usually measured during a specified, finite period of time. Measurement of _____ can be used

- to determine a project's rate of return or value. The time of _____ s into and out of projects are used as inputs in financial models such as internal rate of return, and net present value.
- to determine problems with a business's liquidity. Being profitable does not necessarily mean being liquid. A company can fail because of a shortage of cash, even while profitable.
- as an alternate measure of a business's profits when it is believed that accrual accounting concepts do not represent economic realities. For example, a company may be notionally profitable but generating little operational cash (as may be the case for a company that barters its products rather than selling for cash.) In such a case, the company may be deriving additional operating cash by issuing shares evaluating default risk, re-investment requirements, etc.

_____ is a generic term used differently depending on the context. It may be defined by users for their own purposes.

a. Sweat equity
b. Gross profit
c. Cash flow
d. Gross profit margin

Chapter 10. Flow-Control: Eliminating Process Waste

11. A _____ is the system of organizations, people, technology, activities, information and resources involved in moving a product or service from supplier to customer. _____ activities transform natural resources, raw materials and components into a finished product that is delivered to the end customer. In sophisticated _____ systems, used products may re-enter the _____ at any point where residual value is recyclable.
   a. Supply chain
   b. Drop shipping
   c. Wholesalers
   d. Packaging

12. _____ is the management of a network of interconnected businesses involved in the ultimate provision of product and service packages required by end customers (Harland, 1996.) _____ spans all movement and storage of raw materials, work-in-process inventory, and finished goods from point of origin to point of consumption (supply chain.)

   The definition an American professional association put forward is that _____ encompasses the planning and management of all activities involved in sourcing, procurement, conversion, and logistics management activities.

   a. Supply chain management
   b. Freight forwarder
   c. Drop shipping
   d. Packaging

13. _____ is an inventory strategy that strives to improve the return on investment of a business by reducing in-process inventory and its associated carrying costs. To meet _____ objectives, the process relies on signals between different points in the process. This means the process is often driven by a series of signals, or Kanban, which tell production when to make the next part. Kanban are usually 'tickets' but can be simple visual signals, such as the presence or absence of a part on a shelf. Implemented correctly, _____ can dramatically improve a manufacturing organization's return on investment, quality, and efficiency.
   a. 28-hour day
   b. 33 Strategies of War
   c. 1990 Clean Air Act
   d. Just-in-time

14. _____ is a concept related to lean and just-in-time (JIT) production. The Japanese word _____ is a common term meaning 'signboard' or 'billboard'. According to Taiichi Ohno, the man credited with developing JIT, _____ is a means through which JIT is achieved.

Chapter 10. Flow-Control: Eliminating Process Waste 75

a. Trademark
b. Succession planning
c. Kanban
d. Risk management

15. _____ is the management of the flow of goods, information and other resources, including energy and people, between the point of origin and the point of consumption in order to meet the requirements of consumers (frequently, and originally, military organizations.) _____ involves the integration of information, transportation, inventory, warehousing, material-handling, and packaging, and occasionally security. _____ is a channel of the supply chain which adds the value of time and place utility.
   a. 1990 Clean Air Act
   b. Third-party logistics
   c. 28-hour day
   d. Logistics

16. _____ is one of the four elements of marketing mix. An organization or set of organizations (go-betweens) involved in the process of making a product or service available for use or consumption by a consumer or business user.

The other three parts of the marketing mix are product, pricing, and promotion.

   a. Missing completely at random
   b. Distribution
   c. Job creation programs
   d. Matching theory

17. A _____ for a set of products is a warehouse or other specialized building, often with refrigeration or air conditioning, which is stocked with products (goods) to be re-distributed to retailers, wholesalers or directly to consumers. A _____ is a principle part, the 'order processing' element, of the entire 'order fulfillment' process. _____s are usually thought of as being 'demand driven'.
   a. 1990 Clean Air Act
   b. Distribution center
   c. 28-hour day
   d. Third-party logistics

18. _____ is a practice in logistics of unloading materials from an incoming semi-trailer truck or rail car and loading these materials directly into outbound trucks, trailers with little or no storage in between. This may be done to change type of conveyance, to sort material intended for different destinations or similar destination.

Chapter 10. Flow-Control: Eliminating Process Waste

Cross-Dock operations were first pioneered in the US trucking industry in the 1930's, and have been in continuous use in LTL (less than truckload) operations ever since.

a. Product life cycle
b. Small business
c. Cross-docking
d. Corporate recovery

19. A _____ is the period of time between the initiation of any process of production and the completion of that process. Thus the _____ for ordering a new car from a manufacturer may be anywhere from 2 weeks to 6 months. In industry, _____ reduction is an important part of lean manufacturing.

a. Lead time
b. 33 Strategies of War
c. 1990 Clean Air Act
d. 28-hour day

20. The _____ is an equation that equals the cost of goods sold divided by the average inventory. Average inventory equals beginning inventory plus ending inventory divided by 2.

The formula for _____:

[image]

The formula for average inventory:

[image]

A low turnover rate may point to overstocking, obsolescence, or deficiencies in the product line or marketing effort.

a. Inventory turnover
b. A Stake in the Outcome
c. A4e
d. Asset turnover

21. _____ is an advertisement in which a particular product specifically mentions a competitor by name for the express purpose of showing why the competitor is inferior to the product naming it.

Chapter 10. Flow-Control: Eliminating Process Waste

This should not be confused with parody advertisements, where a fictional product is being advertised for the purpose of poking fun at the particular advertisement, nor should it be confused with the use of a coined brand name for the purpose of comparing the product without actually naming an actual competitor. ('Wikipedia tastes better and is less filling than the Encyclopedia Galactica.')

In the 1980s, during what has been referred to as the cola wars, soft-drink manufacturer Pepsi ran a series of advertisements where people, caught on hidden camera, in a blind taste test, chose Pepsi over rival Coca-Cola.

a. 1990 Clean Air Act
b. 28-hour day
c. 33 Strategies of War
d. Comparative advertising

22. In a human resources context, _____ or labor _____ is the rate at which an employer gains and loses employees. Simple ways to describe it are 'how long employees tend to stay' or 'the rate of traffic through the revolving door.' _____ is measured for individual companies and for their industry as a whole. If an employer is said to have a high _____ relative to its competitors, it means that employees of that company have a shorter average tenure than those of other companies in the same industry.
   a. Ten year occupational employment projection
   b. Career portfolios
   c. Continuous
   d. Turnover

23. _____ are goods that have completed the manufacturing process but have not yet been sold or distributed to the end user.

Manufacturing has three classes of inventory:

1. Raw material
2. Work in process
3. _____

A good purchased as a 'raw material' goes into the manufacture of a product. A good only partially completed during the manufacturing process is called 'work in process'. When the good is completed as to manufacturing but not yet sold or distributed to the end-user is called a 'finished good'.

a. 28-hour day
b. 1990 Clean Air Act
c. Reorder point
d. Finished goods

Chapter 11. Timing-Another Imperative

1. _____ is an area of business concerned with the production of goods and services, and involves the responsibility of ensuring that business operations are efficient in terms of using as little resource as needed, and effective in terms of meeting customer requirements. It is concerned with managing the process that converts inputs (in the forms of materials, labour and energy) into outputs (in the form of goods and services.)

Operations traditionally refers to the production of goods and services separately, although the distinction between these two main types of operations is increasingly difficult to make as manufacturers tend to merge product and service offerings.

   a. A4e
   b. A Stake in the Outcome
   c. AAAI
   d. Operations management

2. _____ is a term defined by the Oxford English Dictionary as an individual's 'course or progress through life '. It is usually considered to pertain to remunerative work (and sometimes also formal education.)

The etymology of the term is somewhat ironic in that it comes from the Latin word carrera, which means race .

   a. Nursing shortage
   b. Career
   c. Spatial mismatch
   d. Career planning

3. A _____ is the period of time between the initiation of any process of production and the completion of that process. Thus the _____ for ordering a new car from a manufacturer may be anywhere from 2 weeks to 6 months. In industry, _____ reduction is an important part of lean manufacturing.
   a. 28-hour day
   b. 33 Strategies of War
   c. 1990 Clean Air Act
   d. Lead time

4. _____ is an advertisement in which a particular product specifically mentions a competitor by name for the express purpose of showing why the competitor is inferior to the product naming it.

This should not be confused with parody advertisements, where a fictional product is being advertised for the purpose of poking fun at the particular advertisement, nor should it be confused with the use of a coined brand name for the purpose of comparing the product without actually naming an actual competitor. ('Wikipedia tastes better and is less filling than the Encyclopedia Galactica.')

Chapter 11. Timing-Another Imperative

In the 1980s, during what has been referred to as the cola wars, soft-drink manufacturer Pepsi ran a series of advertisements where people, caught on hidden camera, in a blind taste test, chose Pepsi over rival Coca-Cola.

a. 33 Strategies of War
b. 28-hour day
c. 1990 Clean Air Act
d. Comparative advertising

5. In business, _____ is a performance metric used to measure the customer service in a supply organization. One example of a _____ measures the number of units filled as a percentage of the total ordered and is known as fill rate. If customer orders total 1000 units, and you can only meet 900 units of that order, your fill rate is 90%.

- In statistics, notably in queuing theory, _____ denotes the rate at which customers are being served in a system. It is the reciprocal of the service time. For example, a supermarket cash desk with an average service time of 30 seconds per customer would have an average _____ of 2 per minute. In statistics the greek letter >μ is used for the _____.

a. Service rate
b. 28-hour day
c. Customer service
d. 1990 Clean Air Act

6. Procter is a surname, and may also refer to:

- Bryan Waller Procter (pseud. Barry Cornwall), English poet
- Goodwin Procter, American law firm
- _____, consumer products multinational

a. Master and Servant Acts
b. Procter ' Gamble
c. Downstream
d. Strict liability

7. _____ is a concept related to lean and just-in-time (JIT) production. The Japanese word _____ is a common term meaning 'signboard' or 'billboard'. According to Taiichi Ohno, the man credited with developing JIT, _____ is a means through which JIT is achieved.

a. Kanban
b. Succession planning
c. Risk management
d. Trademark

8. _____ is the science, art and technology of enclosing or protecting products for distribution, storage, sale, and use. _____ also refers to the process of design, evaluation, and production of packages. _____ can be described as a coordinated system of preparing goods for transport, warehousing, logistics, sale, and end use.

   a. Supply chain
   b. Supply chain management
   c. Wholesalers
   d. Packaging

9. _____ is one of the managerial functions like planning, organizing, staffing and directing. It is an important function because it helps to check the errors and to take the corrective action so that deviation from standards are minimized and stated goals of the organization are achieved in desired manner. According to modern concepts, _____ is a foreseeing action whereas earlier concept of _____ was used only when errors were detected. _____ in management means setting standards, measuring actual performance and taking corrective action.

   a. Turnover
   b. Control
   c. Decision tree pruning
   d. Schedule of reinforcement

10. A _____ is typically described as a deliberate plan of action to guide decisions and achieve rational outcome(s.) However, the term may also be used to denote what is actually done, even though it is unplanned.

The term may apply to government, private sector organizations and groups, and individuals.

   a. Policy
   b. 1990 Clean Air Act
   c. 33 Strategies of War
   d. 28-hour day

11. _____ is a Japanese philosophy that focuses on continuous improvement throughout all aspects of life. When applied to the workplace, _____ activities continually improve all functions of a business, from manufacturing to management and from the CEO to the assembly line workers. By improving standardized activities and processes, _____ aims to eliminate waste.

a. Sensitivity analysis
b. Psychological pricing
c. Cross-docking
d. Kaizen

12. In probability theory, a probability distribution is called _____ if its cumulative distribution function is _____. This is equivalent to saying that for random variables X with the distribution in question, Pr[X = a] = 0 for all real numbers a, i.e.: the probability that X attains the value a is zero, for any number a. If the distribution of X is _____ then X is called a _____ random variable.

a. Continuous
b. Connectionist expert systems
c. Decision tree pruning
d. Pay Band

13. _____ is a management process whereby delivery (customer valued) processes are constantly evaluated and improved in the light of their efficiency, effectiveness and flexibility.

Some see it as a meta process for most management systems (Business Process Management, Quality Management, Project Management). Deming saw it as part of the 'system' whereby feedback from the process and customer were evaluated against organisational goals.

a. Critical Success Factor
b. Sole proprietorship
c. First-mover advantage
d. Continuous Improvement Process

14. _____: A distribution term that refers to the status of items on a purchase order in the event that some or all of the inventory required to fulfill the order is insufficient to satisfy demand. This differs from a forward order where stock is available but delivery is postponed for another reason.

_____ Cost: A cost incurred by a business when it is unable to fill an order and must complete it later.

a. Backorder
b. Mass market
c. Chief analytics officer
d. Chief privacy officer

15. The term '_____' refers to the concept of collecting information and attempting to spot a pattern in the information. In some fields of study, the term '_____' has more formally-defined meanings.

In project management _____ is a mathematical technique that uses historical results to predict future outcome.

   a. Trend analysis
   b. Least squares
   c. Regression analysis
   d. Stepwise regression

Chapter 12. People Demand Productivity

1. The _____ was an evolution of developed countries from an industrial/manufacturing-based wealth producing economy into a service sector asset based economy, brought about by globalization and currency manipulation by governments and their central banks. Some analysts claimed that this change in the economic structure of the United States had created a state of permanent steady growth, low unemployment, and immunity to boom and bust macroeconomic cycles. They believed that the change rendered obsolete many business practices.
   a. 33 Strategies of War
   b. 28-hour day
   c. 1990 Clean Air Act
   d. New economy

2. _____ refers to metrics and measures of output from production processes, per unit of input. Labor _____, for example, is typically measured as a ratio of output per labor-hour, an input. _____ may be conceived of as a metrics of the technical or engineering efficiency of production.
   a. Master production schedule
   b. Value engineering
   c. Remanufacturing
   d. Productivity

3. The _____ is the labour pool in employment. It is generally used to describe those working for a single company or industry, but can also apply to a geographic region like a city, country, state, etc. The term generally excludes the employers or management, and implies those involved in manual labour.
   a. Workforce
   b. Division of labour
   c. Pink-collar worker
   d. Work-life balance

4. In economics, business, retail, and accounting, a _____ is the value of money that has been used up to produce something, and hence is not available for use anymore. In economics, a _____ is an alternative that is given up as a result of a decision. In business, the _____ may be one of acquisition, in which case the amount of money expended to acquire it is counted as _____.
   a. Fixed costs
   b. Cost overrun
   c. Cost
   d. Cost allocation

Chapter 12. People Demand Productivity

5. _____ is an increasingly broadening term with which an organization, or other human system describes the combination of traditionally administrative personnel functions with acquisition and application of skills, knowledge and experience, Employee Relations and resource planning at various levels. The field draws upon concepts developed in Industrial/Organizational Psychology and System Theory. _____ has at least two related interpretations depending on context. The original usage derives from political economy and economics, where it was traditionally called labor, one of four factors of production although this perspective is changing as a function of new and ongoing research into more strategic approaches at national levels. This first usage is used more in terms of '_____ development', and can go beyond just organizations to the level of nations . The more traditional usage within corporations and businesses refers to the individuals within a firm or agency, and to the portion of the organization that deals with hiring, firing, training, and other personnel issues, typically referred to as `_____ management'.
   a. Human resources
   b. Human resource management
   c. Bradford Factor
   d. Progressive discipline

6. In economics and sociology, an _____ is any factor (financial or non-financial) that enables or motivates a particular course of action, or counts as a reason for preferring one choice to the alternatives. It is an expectation that encourages people to behave in a certain way. Since human beings are purposeful creatures, the study of _____ structures is central to the study of all economic activity (both in terms of individual decision-making and in terms of co-operation and competition within a larger institutional structure.)
   a. A Stake in the Outcome
   b. Incentive
   c. AAAI
   d. A4e

7. An _____ is a comprehensive report on a company's activities throughout the preceding year. _____s are intended to give shareholders and other interested persons information about the company's activities and financial performance. Most jurisdictions require companies to prepare and disclose _____s, and many require the _____ to be filed at the company's registry.
   a. AAAI
   b. A Stake in the Outcome
   c. Annual report
   d. A4e

8. _____ is a theory of management that analyzes and synthesizes workflows, with the objective of improving labour productivity. The core ideas of the theory were developed by Frederick Winslow Taylor in the 1880s and 1890s, and were first published in his monographs, Shop Management and The Principles of _____ Taylor believed that decisions based upon tradition and rules of thumb should be replaced by precise procedures developed after careful study of an individual at work.

a. Value engineering
b. Master production schedule
c. Capacity planning
d. Scientific management

9. _____, widely known as F. W. Taylor, was an American mechanical engineer who sought to improve industrial efficiency. He is regarded as the father of scientific management, and was one of the first management consultants.

Taylor was one of the intellectual leaders of the Efficiency Movement and his ideas, broadly conceived, were highly influential in the Progressive Era.

a. Jonah Jacob Goldberg
b. Douglas N. Daft
c. Geoffrey Colvin
d. Frederick Winslow Taylor

10. The _____ is a monograph published by Frederick Winslow Taylor in 1911. This influential monograph is the basis of modern organization and decision theory and has motivated administrators and students of managerial technique. Taylor was an American mechanical engineer and a management consultant in his later years.
a. 1990 Clean Air Act
b. 33 Strategies of War
c. 28-hour day
d. Principles of Scientific management

11. _____ is an advertisement in which a particular product specifically mentions a competitor by name for the express purpose of showing why the competitor is inferior to the product naming it.

This should not be confused with parody advertisements, where a fictional product is being advertised for the purpose of poking fun at the particular advertisement, nor should it be confused with the use of a coined brand name for the purpose of comparing the product without actually naming an actual competitor. ('Wikipedia tastes better and is less filling than the Encyclopedia Galactica.')

In the 1980s, during what has been referred to as the cola wars, soft-drink manufacturer Pepsi ran a series of advertisements where people, caught on hidden camera, in a blind taste test, chose Pepsi over rival Coca-Cola.

a. 1990 Clean Air Act
b. 28-hour day
c. 33 Strategies of War
d. Comparative advertising

12. In organizational development (OD), _____ is the application of Socio-Technical Systems principles and techniques to the humanization of work.

The aims of _____ to improved job satisfaction, to improved through-put, to improved quality and to reduced employee problems, e.g., grievances, absenteeism.

Under scientific management people would be directed by reason and the problems of industrial unrest would be appropriately (i.e., scientifically) addressed.

a. Work design
b. Management process
c. Path-goal theory
d. Graduate recruitment

13. _____ is a technical term used in management science popularized by Joseph M. Juran

He defined an internal and external customers as anyone affected by the product or by the process used to produce the product, in the context of quality management. _____s may play the role as supplier, processer, and customer in the sequence of product development.

He claimed that the organization must understand and identify both internal and external customers and their needs.

a. AAAI
b. A Stake in the Outcome
c. A4e
d. Internal customer

14. _____ means increasing the scope of a job through extending the range of its job duties and responsibilities. This contradicts the principles of specialisation and the division of labour whereby work is divided into small units, each of which is performed repetitively by an individual worker. Some motivational theories suggest that the boredom and alienation caused by the division of labour can actually cause efficiency to fall.

a. Delayering
b. Mock interview
c. Job enlargement
d. Centralization

15. _____ is an attempt to motivate employees by giving them the opportunity to use the range of their abilities. It is an idea that was developed by the American psychologist Frederick Herzberg in the 1950s. It can be contrasted to job enlargement which simply increases the number of tasks without changing the challenge.
a. C-A-K-E
b. Catfish effect
c. Cash cow
d. Job enrichment

16. A _____ is the period of time between the initiation of any process of production and the completion of that process. Thus the _____ for ordering a new car from a manufacturer may be anywhere from 2 weeks to 6 months. In industry, _____ reduction is an important part of lean manufacturing.
a. 1990 Clean Air Act
b. 33 Strategies of War
c. Lead time
d. 28-hour day

17. In organizational development (OD), _____ is a series of actions taken by a Process Owner to identify, analyze and improve existing processes within an organization to meet new goals and objectives. These actions often follow a specific methodology or strategy to create successful results. A sampling of these are listed below.
a. Product innovation
b. Supervisory board
c. Process improvement
d. Letter of resignation

18. _____ and benefits in kind are various non-wage compensations provided to employees in addition to their normal wages or salaries. Where an employee exchanges (cash) wages for some other form of benefit, this is generally referred to as a 'salary sacrifice' arrangement. In most countries, most kinds of _____ are taxable to at least some degree.

a. Employee benefits
b. Interactive Accommodation Process
c. A4e
d. A Stake in the Outcome

19. In business, overhead, _____ or overhead expense refers to an ongoing expense of operating a business. The term overhead is usually used to group expenses that are necessary to the continued functioning of the business, but do not directly generate profits.

Overhead expenses are all costs on the income statement except for direct labor and direct materials.

a. Intangible assets
b. Interlocking directorate
c. Industrial market segmentation
d. Overhead cost

20. In queueing theory, _____ is the proportion of the system's resources which is used by the traffic which arrives at it. It should be strictly less than one for the system to function well. It is usually represented by the symbol ρ.
a. Utilization
b. A4e
c. A Stake in the Outcome
d. AAAI

21. A _____ is a process in which a potential employee is evaluated by an employer for prospective employment in their company, organization and was established in the late 16th century.

A _____ typically precedes the hiring decision, and is used to evaluate the candidate. The interview is usually preceded by the evaluation of submitted résumés from interested candidates, then selecting a small number of candidates for interviews.

a. Payrolling
b. Split shift
c. Supported employment
d. Job interview

Chapter 12. People Demand Productivity

22. _____ is a contract between two parties, one being the employer and the other being the employee. An employee may be defined as: 'A person in the service of another under any contract of hire, express or implied, oral or written, where the employer has the power or right to control and direct the employee in the material details of how the work is to be performed.' Black's Law Dictionary page 471 (5th ed. 1979.)

   a. Exit interview
   b. Employment counsellor
   c. Employment rate
   d. Employment

23. The term '_____' refers to the concept of collecting information and attempting to spot a pattern in the information. In some fields of study, the term '_____' has more formally-defined meanings.

   In project management _____ is a mathematical technique that uses historical results to predict future outcome.

   a. Regression analysis
   b. Stepwise regression
   c. Trend analysis
   d. Least squares

24. _____ is the management of the flow of goods, information and other resources, including energy and people, between the point of origin and the point of consumption in order to meet the requirements of consumers (frequently, and originally, military organizations.) _____ involves the integration of information, transportation, inventory, warehousing, material-handling, and packaging, and occasionally security. _____ is a channel of the supply chain which adds the value of time and place utility.

   a. 1990 Clean Air Act
   b. Third-party logistics
   c. Logistics
   d. 28-hour day

25. _____ generally refers to a list of all planned expenses and revenues. It is a plan for saving and spending. A _____ is an important concept in microeconomics, which uses a _____ line to illustrate the trade-offs between two or more goods.

   a. 1990 Clean Air Act
   b. 33 Strategies of War
   c. 28-hour day
   d. Budget

Chapter 12. People Demand Productivity

26. A time and motion study (or time-motion study) is a business efficiency technique combining the _____ work of Frederick Winslow Taylor with the Motion Study work of Frank and Lillian Gilbreth (not to be confused with their son, best known through the biographical 1950 film and book Cheaper by the Dozen.) It is a major part of scientific management (Taylorism.)

A time and motion study would be used to reduce the number of motions in performing a task in order to increase productivity.

   a. 28-hour day
   b. 1990 Clean Air Act
   c. 33 Strategies of War
   d. Time study

27. _____ is a predetermined motion time system that is used primarily in industrial settings to analyse the methods used to perform any manual operation or task and, as a byproduct of that analysis, set the standard time in which a worker should complete that task.

The basic MTM data was developed by HB Maynard, JL Schwab and GJ Stegemerten of the Methods Engineering Council during a consultancy assignment at the Westinghouse Brake and Signal Corporation, USA in the 1940s. This data and the application rules for the MTM system were refined, extended, defined, industrially tested and documented as a result of further work in later years.

   a. Productivity
   b. Scientific management
   c. Piece rate
   d. Methods-Time Measurement

Chapter 13. Managing Materials: Timing and Quantities

1. In economics, _____ is the total demand for final goods and services in the economy (Y) at a given time and price level. It is the amount of goods and services in the economy that will be purchased at all possible price levels. This is the demand for the gross domestic product of a country when inventory levels are static.

    a. A4e
    b. A Stake in the Outcome
    c. AAAI
    d. Aggregate demand

2. _____ are goods that have completed the manufacturing process but have not yet been sold or distributed to the end user.

Manufacturing has three classes of inventory:

1. Raw material
2. Work in process
3. _____

A good purchased as a 'raw material' goes into the manufacture of a product. A good only partially completed during the manufacturing process is called 'work in process'. When the good is completed as to manufacturing but not yet sold or distributed to the end-user is called a 'finished good'.

   a. 28-hour day
   b. 1990 Clean Air Act
   c. Reorder point
   d. Finished goods

3. The _____ is an equation that equals the cost of goods sold divided by the average inventory. Average inventory equals beginning inventory plus ending inventory divided by 2.

The formula for _____:

The formula for average inventory:

A low turnover rate may point to overstocking, obsolescence, or deficiencies in the product line or marketing effort.

Chapter 13. Managing Materials: Timing and Quantities

a. A4e
b. A Stake in the Outcome
c. Asset turnover
d. Inventory turnover

4. _____ is one of the Accounting Liquidity ratios, a financial ratio. This ratio measures the number of times, on average, the inventory is sold during the period. Its purpose is to measure the liquidity of the inventory.

a. A4e
b. A Stake in the Outcome
c. Inventory
d. Inventory turnover ratio

5. _____ is the branch of logistics that deals with the tangible components of a supply chain. Specifically, this covers the acquisition of spare parts and replacements, quality control of purchasing and ordering such parts, and the standards involved in ordering, shipping, and warehousing the said parts.

A large component of _____ is ensuring that parts and materials used in the supply chain meet minimum requirements by performing quality assurance (QA.)

a. Supply-Chain Operations Reference
b. Delayed differentiation
c. Vendor Managed Inventory
d. Materials management

6. _____: A distribution term that refers to the status of items on a purchase order in the event that some or all of the inventory required to fulfill the order is insufficient to satisfy demand. This differs from a forward order where stock is available but delivery is postponed for another reason.

_____ Cost: A cost incurred by a business when it is unable to fill an order and must complete it later.

a. Chief privacy officer
b. Chief analytics officer
c. Mass market
d. Backorder

Chapter 13. Managing Materials: Timing and Quantities

7. The '_____ scheme' is an economic term, referring to the use of commodity storage for economic stabilization. Specifically, commodities are bought and stored when there is a surplus in the economy and they are sold from these stores when there are shortages in the economy. The institutional buying, storing and selling of commodities by a large player (e.g. a government) can take place for one commodity or a 'basket of commodities'.

   a. Power
   b. Reservation wage
   c. Contingent employment
   d. Buffer stock

8. In economics, _____ is the desire to own something and the ability to pay for it. The term _____ signifies the ability or the willingness to buy a particular commodity at a given point of time.

   a. 1990 Clean Air Act
   b. 28-hour day
   c. 33 Strategies of War
   d. Demand

9. In a human resources context, _____ or labor _____ is the rate at which an employer gains and loses employees. Simple ways to describe it are 'how long employees tend to stay' or 'the rate of traffic through the revolving door.' _____ is measured for individual companies and for their industry as a whole. If an employer is said to have a high _____ relative to its competitors, it means that employees of that company have a shorter average tenure than those of other companies in the same industry.

   a. Ten year occupational employment projection
   b. Continuous
   c. Turnover
   d. Career portfolios

10. The _____ is the level of inventory when a fresh order should be made with suppliers to bring the inventory up by the Economic order quantity ('EOQ'.)

    The _____ for replenishment of stock occurs when the level of inventory drops down to zero. In view of instantaneous replenishment of stock the level of inventory jumps to the original level from zero level.

    a. Reorder point
    b. 1990 Clean Air Act
    c. 28-hour day
    d. Finished goods

11. _____ is the provision of service to customers before, during and after a purchase.

Chapter 13. Managing Materials: Timing and Quantities

According to Turban et al. (2002), '_____ is a series of activities designed to enhance the level of customer satisfaction - that is, the feeling that a product or service has met the customer expectation.'

Its importance varies by product, industry and customer; defective or broken merchandise can be exchanged, often only with a receipt and within a specified time frame.

a. 1990 Clean Air Act
b. 28-hour day
c. Customer service
d. Service rate

12. _____ is an advertisement in which a particular product specifically mentions a competitor by name for the express purpose of showing why the competitor is inferior to the product naming it.

This should not be confused with parody advertisements, where a fictional product is being advertised for the purpose of poking fun at the particular advertisement, nor should it be confused with the use of a coined brand name for the purpose of comparing the product without actually naming an actual competitor. ('Wikipedia tastes better and is less filling than the Encyclopedia Galactica.')

In the 1980s, during what has been referred to as the cola wars, soft-drink manufacturer Pepsi ran a series of advertisements where people, caught on hidden camera, in a blind taste test, chose Pepsi over rival Coca-Cola.

a. 28-hour day
b. 33 Strategies of War
c. Comparative advertising
d. 1990 Clean Air Act

13. _____ measures the performance of a system. Certain goals are defined and the _____ gives the percentage to which they should be achieved.

Examples

- Percentage of calls answered in a call center.
- Percentage of customers waiting less than a given fixed time.
- Percentage of customers that do not experience a stock out.

_____ is used in supply chain management and in inventory management to measure the performance of inventory systems.

Chapter 13. Managing Materials: Timing and Quantities

Under stochastic conditions it is unavoidable that in some periods the inventory on hand is not sufficient to deliver the complete demand and, as a consequence, that part of the demand is filled only after an inventory-related waiting time.

a. 1990 Clean Air Act
b. Service level
c. 33 Strategies of War
d. 28-hour day

14. _____ is a term used by inventory specialists to describe a level of extra stock that is maintained below the cycle stock to buffer against stockouts. _____ exists to counter uncertainties in supply and demand. _____ is defined as extra units of inventory carried as protection against possible stockouts .(shortfall in raw material or packaging.)

a. Product life cycle
b. Knowledge worker
c. Process automation
d. Safety stock

15. In economics, business, retail, and accounting, a _____ is the value of money that has been used up to produce something, and hence is not available for use anymore. In economics, a _____ is an alternative that is given up as a result of a decision. In business, the _____ may be one of acquisition, in which case the amount of money expended to acquire it is counted as _____.

a. Fixed costs
b. Cost overrun
c. Cost allocation
d. Cost

16. _____ is the state of being which occurs when a person, object, or service is no longer wanted even though it may still be in good working order. _____ frequently occurs because a replacement has become available that is superior in one or more aspects. Videotapes making way for DVDs

Technical _____ may occur when a new product or technology supersedes the old, and it becomes preferred to utilize the new technology in place of the old.

a. Obsolescence
b. A4e
c. A Stake in the Outcome
d. AAAI

Chapter 13. Managing Materials: Timing and Quantities

17. _____ is the level of inventory that minimizes the total inventory holding costs and ordering costs. The framework used to determine this order quantity is also known as Wilson _____ Model. The model was developed by F. W. Harris in 1913.

   a. Event management
   b. Anti-leadership
   c. Effective executive
   d. Economic order quantity

18. _____ is a list of the raw materials, sub-assemblies, intermediate assemblies, sub-components, components, parts and the quantities of each needed to manufacture an end item (final product).

   a. Bill of materials
   b. Methods-time measurement
   c. Piece rate
   d. Scientific management

19. _____ is a software based production planning and inventory control system used to manage manufacturing processes. Although it is not common nowadays, it is possible to conduct _____ by hand as well.

   An _____ system is intended to simultaneously meet three objectives:

   - Ensure materials and products are available for production and delivery to customers.
   - Maintain the lowest possible level of inventory.
   - Plan manufacturing activities, delivery schedules and purchasing activities.

   Manufacturing organizations, whatever their products, face the same daily practical problem - that customers want products to be available in a shorter time than it takes to make them. This means that some level of planning is required.

   a. 33 Strategies of War
   b. 28-hour day
   c. Material requirements planning
   d. 1990 Clean Air Act

20. In general, _____ means to allow a positive value and a negative value to set-off and partially or entirely cancel each other out.

Chapter 13. Managing Materials: Timing and Quantities

In the context of credit risk, there are at least three specific types of _____:

- Close-out _____: In the event of counterparty bankruptcy or any other relevant event of default specified in the relevant agreement which if accelerated (i.e. effected), all transactions or all of a given type are netted (i.e. set off against each other) at market value or if otherwise specified in the contract or if it is not possible to obtain a market value at an amount equal to the loss suffered by the non-defaulting party in replacing the relevant contract. The alternative would allow the liquidator to choose which contracts to enforce and which not to (and thus potentially 'cherry pick'.) There are international jurisdictions where the enforceability of _____ in bankruptcy has not been legally tested.

- _____ by novation: The legal obligations of the parties to make required payments under one or more series of related transactions are canceled and a new obligation to make only the net payments is created.

- Settlement or payment _____: For cash settled trades, this can be applied either bilaterally or multilaterally and on related or unrelated transactions.

_____ decreases credit exposure, increases business with existing counterparties, and reduces both operational and settlement risk and operational costs.

In the context of pollution control, _____ refers to a procedure whereby a company can create a new pollution source only if it makes equal reductions in pollution elsewhere in the company, i.e. it cannot acquire new permits from the outside.

a. Netting
b. Market value added
c. Deferred compensation
d. Net worth

21. In mathematical logic, _____ is a valid argument and rule of inference which makes the inference that, if the conjunction A and B is true, then A is true, and B is true.

In formal language:

$$A \wedge B \vdash A$$

or

$$A \wedge B \vdash B$$

Chapter 13. Managing Materials: Timing and Quantities

The argument has one premise, namely a conjunction, and one often uses _____ in longer arguments to derive one of the conjuncts.

An example in English:

It's raining and it's pouring.

a. Fuzzy logic
b. 1990 Clean Air Act
c. Validity
d. Simplification

22. A _____ is a plan for production, staffing, inventory, etc. It is usually linked to manufacturing where the plan indicates when and how much of each product will be demanded. This plan quantifies significant processes, parts, and other resources in order to optimize production, to identify bottlenecks, and to anticipate needs and completed goods.
   a. Remanufacturing
   b. Master production schedule
   c. Value engineering
   d. Piecework

23. _____ is one of the four elements of marketing mix. An organization or set of organizations (go-betweens) involved in the process of making a product or service available for use or consumption by a consumer or business user.

The other three parts of the marketing mix are product, pricing, and promotion.

   a. Distribution
   b. Job creation programs
   c. Missing completely at random
   d. Matching theory

24. _____ is defined by APICS as a method for the effective planning of all resources of a manufacturing company. Ideally, it addresses operational planning in units, financial planning in dollars, and has a simulation capability to answer 'what-if' questions and extension of closed-loop _____. Manufacturing resource planning (or Manufacturing resource planning2) - Around 1980, over-frequent changes in sales forecasts, entailing continual readjustments in production, as well as the unsuitability of the parameters fixed by the system, led _____ (Material Requirement Planning) to evolve into a new concept : _____ (e.g. _____ 2)

This is not exclusively a software function, but a marriage of people skills, dedication to data base accuracy, and computer resources.

Chapter 13. Managing Materials: Timing and Quantities

a. Homeworkers
b. MRP II
c. Jidoka
d. Manufacturing resource planning

25. _____ is a company-wide computer software system used to manage and coordinate all the resources, information, and functions of a business from shared data stores.

An _____ system has a service-oriented architecture with modular hardware and software units and 'services' that communicate on a local area network. The modular design allows a business to add or reconfigure modules (perhaps from different vendors) while preserving data integrity in one shared database that may be centralized or distributed.

a. A Stake in the Outcome
b. AAAI
c. A4e
d. Enterprise resource planning

26. _____ is the amount of goods and services that a labourer produces in a given amount of time. It is one of several types of productivity that economists measure. _____ can be measured for a firm, a process or a country.

a. Labour productivity
b. Retroactive overtime
c. Business Network Transformation
d. Time and attendance

27. Manufacturing Resource Planning (_____) is defined by APICS as a method for the effective planning of all resources of a manufacturing company. Ideally, it addresses operational planning in units, financial planning in dollars, and has a simulation capability to answer 'what-if' questions and extension of closed-loop MRP. Manufacturing Resource Planning (or MRP2) - Around 1980, over-frequent changes in sales forecasts, entailing continual readjustments in production, as well as the unsuitability of the parameters fixed by the system, led MRP (Material Requirement Planning) to evolve into a new concept : Manufacturing Resource Planning (e.g. MRP 2)

This is not exclusively a software function, but a marriage of people skills, dedication to data base accuracy, and computer resources.

a. MRP II
b. Manufacturing resource planning
c. Homeworkers
d. Jidoka

28. _____ refers to metrics and measures of output from production processes, per unit of input. Labor _____, for example, is typically measured as a ratio of output per labor-hour, an input. _____ may be conceived of as a metrics of the technical or engineering efficiency of production.
a. Value engineering
b. Productivity
c. Master production schedule
d. Remanufacturing

Chapter 13. Managing Materials: Timing and Quantities

29. In microeconomics, industrial organization is the field which describes the behavior of firms in the marketplace with regard to production, pricing, employment and other decisions. _____ in this field range from classical issues such as opportunity cost to neoclassical concepts such as factors of production.

- Production theory basics
    - production efficiency
    - factors of production
    - total, average, and marginal product curves
    - marginal productivity
    - isoquants ' isocosts
    - the marginal rate of technical substitution
- Economic rent
    - classical factor rents
    - Paretian factor rents
- Production possibility frontier
    - what products are possible given a set of resources
    - the trade-off between producing one product rather than another
    - the marginal rate of transformation
- Production function
    - inputs
    - diminishing returns to inputs
    - the stages of production
    - shifts in a production function
- Cost theory
    - the different types of costs
        - opportunity cost
        - accounting cost or historical costs
        - transaction cost
        - sunk cost
        - marginal cost
    - the isocost line
- Cost-of-production theory of value
- Long-run cost and production functions
    - long-run average cost
    - long-run production function and efficiency
    - returns to scale and isoclines
    - minimum efficient scale
    - plant capacity
- Economies of density
- Economies of scale
    - the efficiency consequences of increasing or decreasing the level of production
- Economies of scope
    - the efficiency consequences of increasing or decreasing the number of different types of products produced, promoted, and distributed
- Optimum factor allocation
    - output elasticity of factor costs
    - marginal revenue product
    - marginal resource cost
- Pricing
    - various aspects of the pricing decision
- Transfer pricing
    - selling within a multi-divisional company
- Joint product pricing
    - price setting when two products are linked
- Price discrimination

- - - different prices to different buyers
    - types of price discrimination
    - yield management
- Price skimming
    - price discrimination over time
- Two part tariffs
    - charging a price composed of two parts, usually an initial fee and an ongoing fee
- Price points
    - the effects of a non-linear demand curve on pricing
- Cost-plus pricing
    - a markup is applied to a cost term in order to calculate price
    - cost-plus pricing with elasticity considerations
    - cost plus pricing is often used along with break even analysis
- Rate of return pricing
    - calculate price based on the required rate of return on investment, or rate of return on sales
- Profit maximization
    - determining the optimum price and quantity
    - the totals approach
    - marginal approach of production

a. Markup
b. Price floor
c. Pricing
d. Topics

Chapter 14. Facilities Management

1. An _____ is the negative aspects of human activity on the biophysical environment. Environmentalism, a social and environmental movement that started in the 1960s, focuses on addressing _____s through advocacy, education and activism.

Major current _____s are climate change, pollution and resource depletion.

   a. A4e
   b. A Stake in the Outcome
   c. AAAI
   d. Environmental issue

2. In economics, business, retail, and accounting, a _____ is the value of money that has been used up to produce something, and hence is not available for use anymore. In economics, a _____ is an alternative that is given up as a result of a decision. In business, the _____ may be one of acquisition, in which case the amount of money expended to acquire it is counted as _____.
   a. Cost allocation
   b. Cost overrun
   c. Fixed costs
   d. Cost

3. _____ is one of the four elements of marketing mix. An organization or set of organizations (go-betweens) involved in the process of making a product or service available for use or consumption by a consumer or business user.

The other three parts of the marketing mix are product, pricing, and promotion.

   a. Missing completely at random
   b. Matching theory
   c. Distribution
   d. Job creation programs

4. In queueing theory, _____ is the proportion of the system's resources which is used by the traffic which arrives at it. It should be strictly less than one for the system to function well. It is usually represented by the symbol ρ.
   a. AAAI
   b. A4e
   c. Utilization
   d. A Stake in the Outcome

Chapter 14. Facilities Management

5. An _____ is a manufacturing process in which parts (usually interchangeable parts) are added to a product in a sequential manner using optimally planned logistics to create a finished product much faster than with handcrafting-type methods. The _____ developed by Ford Motor Company between 1908 and 1915 made _____s famous in the following decade through the social ramifications of mass production, such as the affordability of the Ford Model T and the introduction of high wages for Ford workers. However, the various preconditions for the development at Ford stretched far back into the 19th century, from the gradual realization of the dream of interchangeability, to the concept of reinventing workflow and job descriptions using analytical methods.

   a. Assembly line
   b. A4e
   c. AAAI
   d. A Stake in the Outcome

6. _____ is an advertisement in which a particular product specifically mentions a competitor by name for the express purpose of showing why the competitor is inferior to the product naming it.

This should not be confused with parody advertisements, where a fictional product is being advertised for the purpose of poking fun at the particular advertisement, nor should it be confused with the use of a coined brand name for the purpose of comparing the product without actually naming an actual competitor. ('Wikipedia tastes better and is less filling than the Encyclopedia Galactica.')

In the 1980s, during what has been referred to as the cola wars, soft-drink manufacturer Pepsi ran a series of advertisements where people, caught on hidden camera, in a blind taste test, chose Pepsi over rival Coca-Cola.

   a. Comparative advertising
   b. 33 Strategies of War
   c. 1990 Clean Air Act
   d. 28-hour day

7. A _____ is a set of sequential operations established in a factory whereby materials are put through a refining process to produce an end-product that is suitable for onward consumption; or components are assembled to make a finished article.

Typically, raw materials such as metal ores or agricultural products such as foodstuffs or textile source plants (cotton, flax) require a sequence of treatments to render them useful. For metal, the processes include crushing, smelting and further refining.

   a. Six Sigma
   b. Theory of constraints
   c. Production line
   d. Takt time

Chapter 14. Facilities Management

8. _____ has the following meanings:

The care and servicing by personnel for the purpose of maintaining equipment and facilities in satisfactory operating condition by providing for systematic inspection, detection, and correction of incipient failures either before they occur or before they develop into major defects.

1. Maintenance, including tests, measurements, adjustments, and parts replacement, performed specifically to prevent faults from occurring.

While _____ is generally considered to be worthwhile, there are risks such as equipment failure or human error involved when performing _____, just as in any maintenance operation. _____ as scheduled overhaul or scheduled replacement provides two of the three proactive failure management policies available to the maintenance engineer. Common methods of determining what _____ failure management policies should be applied are; OEM recommendations, requirements of codes and legislation within a jurisdiction, what an 'expert' thinks ought to be done, or the maintenance that's already done to similar equipment.

   a. 33 Strategies of War
   b. 1990 Clean Air Act
   c. Preventive maintenance
   d. 28-hour day

9. _____ techniques help determine the condition of in-service equipment in order to predict when maintenance should be performed. This approach offers cost savings over routine or time-based preventive maintenance, because tasks are performed only when warranted.

PdM, or condition-based maintenance, attempts to evaluate the condition of equipment by performing periodic or continuous (online) equipment condition monitoring.

   a. 28-hour day
   b. Reverse engineering
   c. Predictive maintenance
   d. 1990 Clean Air Act

10. _____ occurs when a corporation is owned in whole or in part by its employees. Employees are usually given a share of the corporation after a certain length of employment or they can buy shares at any time. A corporation owned entirely by its employees (such as a worker cooperative) will not, therefore, have its shares sold on public stock markets, often opting instead for mixed ownership arrangements involving a trust.

a. Amoco Corporation
b. Employee ownership
c. Anaconda Copper
d. AT'T Inc.

11. _____ is the state or fact of exclusive rights and control over property, which may be an object, land/real estate or intellectual property. An _____ right is also referred to as title. The concept of _____ has existed for thousands of years and in all cultures.
   a. Emanation of the state
   b. Ownership
   c. A Stake in the Outcome
   d. A4e

12. _____ is a system of intermodal freight transport using standard intermodal containers that are standardised by the International Organization for Standardization (ISO.) These can be loaded and sealed intact onto container ships, railroad cars, planes, and trucks.
   a. 33 Strategies of War
   b. Containerization
   c. 1990 Clean Air Act
   d. 28-hour day

13. _____ is an inventory strategy that strives to improve the return on investment of a business by reducing in-process inventory and its associated carrying costs. To meet _____ objectives, the process relies on signals between different points in the process. This means the process is often driven by a series of signals, or Kanban , which tell production when to make the next part. Kanban are usually 'tickets' but can be simple visual signals, such as the presence or absence of a part on a shelf. Implemented correctly, _____ can dramatically improve a manufacturing organization's return on investment, quality, and efficiency.
   a. 1990 Clean Air Act
   b. Just-in-time
   c. 33 Strategies of War
   d. 28-hour day

Chapter 15. Managing Continuous and Repetitive Operations

1. _____ is used for the design, development, analysis, and optimization of technical processes and is mainly applied to chemical plants and chemical processes, but also to power stations, and similar technical facilities. Process flow diagram of a typical amine treating process used in industrial plants

_____ is a model-based representation of chemical, physical, biological, and other technical processes and unit operations in software. Basic prerequisites are a thorough knowledge of chemical and physical properties of pure components and mixtures, of reactions, and of mathematical models which, in combination, allow the calculation of a process in computers.

   a. 28-hour day
   b. 33 Strategies of War
   c. 1990 Clean Air Act
   d. Process simulation

2. _____ has the following meanings:

The care and servicing by personnel for the purpose of maintaining equipment and facilities in satisfactory operating condition by providing for systematic inspection, detection, and correction of incipient failures either before they occur or before they develop into major defects.

   1. Maintenance, including tests, measurements, adjustments, and parts replacement, performed specifically to prevent faults from occurring.

While _____ is generally considered to be worthwhile, there are risks such as equipment failure or human error involved when performing _____, just as in any maintenance operation. _____ as scheduled overhaul or scheduled replacement provides two of the three proactive failure management policies available to the maintenance engineer. Common methods of determining what _____ failure management policies should be applied are; OEM recommendations, requirements of codes and legislation within a jurisdiction, what an 'expert' thinks ought to be done, or the maintenance that's already done to similar equipment.

   a. 28-hour day
   b. 33 Strategies of War
   c. 1990 Clean Air Act
   d. Preventive maintenance

3. _____ can be defined as the maximum time per unit allowed to produce a product in order to meet demand. It is derived from the German word Taktzeit which translates to cycle time. _____ sets the pace for industrial manufacturing lines. In automobile manufacturing, for example, cars are assembled on a line, and are moved on to the next station after a certain time - the _____. Therefore, the time needed to complete work on each station has to be less than the _____ in order for the product to be completed within the alloted time.

Chapter 15. Managing Continuous and Repetitive Operations

a. Six Sigma
b. Takt time
c. Production line
d. Theory of constraints

4. _____ is a software based production planning and inventory control system used to manage manufacturing processes. Although it is not common nowadays, it is possible to conduct _____ by hand as well.

An _____ system is intended to simultaneously meet three objectives:

- Ensure materials and products are available for production and delivery to customers.
- Maintain the lowest possible level of inventory.
- Plan manufacturing activities, delivery schedules and purchasing activities.

Manufacturing organizations, whatever their products, face the same daily practical problem - that customers want products to be available in a shorter time than it takes to make them. This means that some level of planning is required.

a. 33 Strategies of War
b. 28-hour day
c. 1990 Clean Air Act
d. Material requirements planning

5. _____ is an adjective for experience-based techniques that help in problem solving, learning and discovery. A _____ method is particularly used to rapidly come to a solution that is hoped to be close to the best possible answer, or 'optimal solution'. _____s are 'rules of thumb', educated guesses, intuitive judgments or simply common sense.

a. Heuristic
b. 28-hour day
c. Representativeness
d. 1990 Clean Air Act

6. The _____ Method is a tool for scheduling activities in a project plan. It is a method of constructing a project schedule network diagram that uses boxes, referred to as nodes, to represent activities and connects them with arrows that show the dependencies.

- Critical Tasks, noncritical tasks, and slack time
- Shows the relationship of the tasks to each other
- Allows for what-if, worst-case, best-case and most likely scenario

Key elements include determining predecessors and defining attributes such as

- early start date
- last-last
- early finish date
- late finish date
- Duration
- WBS reference

a. Project manager
b. Project management office
c. Work package
d. Precedence diagram

Chapter 16. Managing Job and Batch Operations

1. _____ is execution of a series of programs ('jobs') on a computer without human interaction.

Batch jobs are set up so they can be run to completion without human interaction, so all input data is preselected through scripts or command-line parameters. This is in contrast to 'online' or interactive programs which prompt the user for such input.

   a. Batch processing
   b. 33 Strategies of War
   c. 1990 Clean Air Act
   d. 28-hour day

2. _____ refers to the movement of cash into or out of a business or financial product. It is usually measured during a specified, finite period of time. Measurement of _____ can be used

   - to determine a project's rate of return or value. The time of _____s into and out of projects are used as inputs in financial models such as internal rate of return, and net present value.
   - to determine problems with a business's liquidity. Being profitable does not necessarily mean being liquid. A company can fail because of a shortage of cash, even while profitable.
   - as an alternate measure of a business's profits when it is believed that accrual accounting concepts do not represent economic realities. For example, a company may be notionally profitable but generating little operational cash (as may be the case for a company that barters its products rather than selling for cash.) In such a case, the company may be deriving additional operating cash by issuing shares evaluating default risk, re-investment requirements, etc.

   _____ is a generic term used differently depending on the context. It may be defined by users for their own purposes.

   a. Gross profit
   b. Gross profit margin
   c. Sweat equity
   d. Cash flow

3. _____ is one of the managerial functions like planning, organizing, staffing and directing. It is an important function because it helps to check the errors and to take the corrective action so that deviation from standards are minimized and stated goals of the organization are achieved in desired manner. According to modern concepts, _____ is a foreseeing action whereas earlier concept of _____ was used only when errors were detected. _____ in management means setting standards, measuring actual performance and taking corrective action.
   a. Control
   b. Decision tree pruning
   c. Turnover
   d. Schedule of reinforcement

Chapter 16. Managing Job and Batch Operations

4. In mathematical logic, _____ is a valid argument and rule of inference which makes the inference that, if the conjunction A and B is true, then A is true, and B is true.

In formal language:

$$A \wedge B \vdash A$$

or

$$A \wedge B \vdash B$$

The argument has one premise, namely a conjunction, and one often uses _____ in longer arguments to derive one of the conjuncts.

An example in English:

It's raining and it's pouring.

a. Fuzzy logic
b. Simplification
c. Validity
d. 1990 Clean Air Act

5. A _____ is a type of bar chart that illustrates a project schedule. _____s illustrate the start and finish dates of the terminal elements and summary elements of a project. Terminal elements and summary elements comprise the work breakdown structure of the project.

a. Gantt chart
b. 1990 Clean Air Act
c. 33 Strategies of War
d. 28-hour day

6. A _____ is the period of time between the initiation of any process of production and the completion of that process. Thus the _____ for ordering a new car from a manufacturer may be anywhere from 2 weeks to 6 months. In industry, _____ reduction is an important part of lean manufacturing.

a. 33 Strategies of War
b. 1990 Clean Air Act
c. Lead time
d. 28-hour day

Chapter 16. Managing Job and Batch Operations

7. _____ is a software based production planning and inventory control system used to manage manufacturing processes. Although it is not common nowadays, it is possible to conduct _____ by hand as well.

An _____ system is intended to simultaneously meet three objectives:

- Ensure materials and products are available for production and delivery to customers.
- Maintain the lowest possible level of inventory.
- Plan manufacturing activities, delivery schedules and purchasing activities.

Manufacturing organizations, whatever their products, face the same daily practical problem - that customers want products to be available in a shorter time than it takes to make them. This means that some level of planning is required.

a. 1990 Clean Air Act
b. 33 Strategies of War
c. 28-hour day
d. Material requirements planning

8. _____, a business term, is a measure of how products and services supplied by a company meet or surpass customer expectation. It is seen as a key performance indicator within business and is part of the four perspectives of a Balanced Scorecard.

In a competitive marketplace where businesses compete for customers, _____ is seen as a key differentiator and increasingly has become a key element of business strategy.

a. Horizontal integration
b. Foreign ownership
c. Critical Success Factor
d. Customer satisfaction

9. In economics, business, retail, and accounting, a _____ is the value of money that has been used up to produce something, and hence is not available for use anymore. In economics, a _____ is an alternative that is given up as a result of a decision. In business, the _____ may be one of acquisition, in which case the amount of money expended to acquire it is counted as _____.
a. Fixed costs
b. Cost allocation
c. Cost overrun
d. Cost

Chapter 16. Managing Job and Batch Operations

10. The _____ is the labour pool in employment. It is generally used to describe those working for a single company or industry, but can also apply to a geographic region like a city, country, state, etc. The term generally excludes the employers or management, and implies those involved in manual labour.
   a. Workforce
   b. Pink-collar worker
   c. Work-life balance
   d. Division of labour

11. _____ are typically small manufacturing operations that handle specialized manufacturing processes such as small customer orders or small batch jobs. _____ typically move on to different jobs (possibly with different customers) when each job is completed. By nature of this type of manufacturing operation, _____ are usually specialized in skill and processes.
   a. 33 Strategies of War
   b. Job shops
   c. 1990 Clean Air Act
   d. 28-hour day

12. _____ is a service policy where by the requests of customers or clients are attended to in the order that they arrived, without other biases or preferences. The policy can be employed when processing sales orders, in determining restaurant seating, or on a taxi stand, for example.

Festival seating (also known as general seating and stadium seating) is seating done on a FCFS basis.

   a. First-come, first-served
   b. 28-hour day
   c. 33 Strategies of War
   d. 1990 Clean Air Act

13. A _____ is a process in which a potential employee is evaluated by an employer for prospective employment in their company, organization and was established in the late 16th century.

A _____ typically precedes the hiring decision, and is used to evaluate the candidate. The interview is usually preceded by the evaluation of submitted résumés from interested candidates, then selecting a small number of candidates for interviews.

Chapter 16. Managing Job and Batch Operations

a. Split shift
b. Supported employment
c. Job interview
d. Payrolling

14. In probability theory, a probability distribution is called _____ if its cumulative distribution function is _____. This is equivalent to saying that for random variables X with the distribution in question, Pr[X = a] = 0 for all real numbers a, i.e.: the probability that X attains the value a is zero, for any number a. If the distribution of X is _____ then X is called a _____ random variable.

a. Decision tree pruning
b. Connectionist expert systems
c. Pay Band
d. Continuous

15. _____ is a management process whereby delivery (customer valued) processes are constantly evaluated and improved in the light of their efficiency, effectiveness and flexibility.

Some see it as a meta process for most management systems (Business Process Management, Quality Management, Project Management). Deming saw it as part of the 'system' whereby feedback from the process and customer were evaluated against organisational goals.

a. Continuous Improvement Process
b. First-mover advantage
c. Sole proprietorship
d. Critical Success Factor

16. _____ is a company-wide computer software system used to manage and coordinate all the resources, information, and functions of a business from shared data stores.

An _____ system has a service-oriented architecture with modular hardware and software units and 'services' that communicate on a local area network. The modular design allows a business to add or reconfigure modules (perhaps from different vendors) while preserving data integrity in one shared database that may be centralized or distributed.

a. Enterprise resource planning
b. A4e
c. A Stake in the Outcome
d. AAAI

17. _____ is a Japanese philosophy that focuses on continuous improvement throughout all aspects of life. When applied to the workplace, _____ activities continually improve all functions of a business, from manufacturing to management and from the CEO to the assembly line workers. By improving standardized activities and processes, _____ aims to eliminate waste .
   a. Psychological pricing
   b. Cross-docking
   c. Sensitivity analysis
   d. Kaizen

Chapter 17. Managing Projects

1. _____ refers to the movement of cash into or out of a business or financial product. It is usually measured during a specified, finite period of time. Measurement of _____ can be used

   - to determine a project's rate of return or value. The time of _____s into and out of projects are used as inputs in financial models such as internal rate of return, and net present value.
   - to determine problems with a business's liquidity. Being profitable does not necessarily mean being liquid. A company can fail because of a shortage of cash, even while profitable.
   - as an alternate measure of a business's profits when it is believed that accrual accounting concepts do not represent economic realities. For example, a company may be notionally profitable but generating little operational cash (as may be the case for a company that barters its products rather than selling for cash.) In such a case, the company may be deriving additional operating cash by issuing shares evaluating default risk, re-investment requirements, etc.

   _____ is a generic term used differently depending on the context. It may be defined by users for their own purposes.

   a. Gross profit
   b. Gross profit margin
   c. Sweat equity
   d. Cash flow

2. _____ is the discipline of planning, organizing and managing resources to bring about the successful completion of specific project goals and objectives. It is often closely related to and sometimes conflated with Program management.

   A project is a finite endeavor--having specific start and completion dates--undertaken to meet particular goals and objectives, usually to bring about beneficial change or added value.

   a. Project management
   b. Work package
   c. Project engineer
   d. Precedence diagram

3. _____ is the process of comparing the cost, cycle time, productivity, or quality of a specific process or method to another that is widely considered to be an industry standard or best practice. Essentially, _____ provides a snapshot of the performance of your business and helps you understand where you are in relation to a particular standard. The result is often a business case for making changes in order to make improvements.
   a. Competitive heterogeneity
   b. Cost leadership
   c. Benchmarking
   d. Complementors

4. An _____ is the negative aspects of human activity on the biophysical environment. Environmentalism, a social and environmental movement that started in the 1960s, focuses on addressing _____s through advocacy, education and activism.

Major current _____s are climate change, pollution and resource depletion.

a. A4e
b. AAAI
c. A Stake in the Outcome
d. Environmental issue

5. In probability theory, a probability distribution is called _____ if its cumulative distribution function is _____. This is equivalent to saying that for random variables X with the distribution in question, Pr[X = a] = 0 for all real numbers a, i.e.: the probability that X attains the value a is zero, for any number a. If the distribution of X is _____ then X is called a _____ random variable.
a. Connectionist expert systems
b. Pay Band
c. Continuous
d. Decision tree pruning

6. _____ is a management process whereby delivery (customer valued) processes are constantly evaluated and improved in the light of their efficiency, effectiveness and flexibility.

Some see it as a meta process for most management systems (Business Process Management, Quality Management, Project Management). Deming saw it as part of the 'system' whereby feedback from the process and customer were evaluated against organisational goals.

a. Sole proprietorship
b. First-mover advantage
c. Critical Success Factor
d. Continuous Improvement Process

7. In economics, _____ is the desire to own something and the ability to pay for it. The term _____ signifies the ability or the willingness to buy a particular commodity at a given point of time.
a. 33 Strategies of War
b. 28-hour day
c. 1990 Clean Air Act
d. Demand

Chapter 17. Managing Projects

8. A _____ is directly responsible for managing the day-to-day operations (and profitability) of a company.

Chief Executive Officer (CEO)
- As the top manager, the CEO is typically responsible for the entire operations of the corporation and reports directly to the chairman and board of directors. It is the CEO's responsibility to implement board decisions and initiatives and to maintain the smooth operation of the firm, with the assistance of senior management.

a. Getting Things Done
b. Field service management
c. Management team
d. Vorstand

9. _____ is an advertisement in which a particular product specifically mentions a competitor by name for the express purpose of showing why the competitor is inferior to the product naming it.

This should not be confused with parody advertisements, where a fictional product is being advertised for the purpose of poking fun at the particular advertisement, nor should it be confused with the use of a coined brand name for the purpose of comparing the product without actually naming an actual competitor. ('Wikipedia tastes better and is less filling than the Encyclopedia Galactica.')

In the 1980s, during what has been referred to as the cola wars, soft-drink manufacturer Pepsi ran a series of advertisements where people, caught on hidden camera, in a blind taste test, chose Pepsi over rival Coca-Cola.

a. 28-hour day
b. 33 Strategies of War
c. 1990 Clean Air Act
d. Comparative advertising

10. A _____ is a name or trademark connected with a product or producer. _____s have become increasingly important components of culture and the economy, now being described as 'cultural accessories and personal philosophies'.

Some people distinguish the psychological aspect of a _____ from the experiential aspect.

a. Brand
b. Brand loyalty
c. Brand extension
d. Brand awareness

Chapter 17. Managing Projects

11. A _____ researches, selects, develops, and places a company's products.

A _____ considers numerous factors such as target demographic, the products offered by the competition, and how well the product fits in with the company's business model. Generally, a _____ manages one or more tangible products.

   a. Product manager
   b. 28-hour day
   c. 33 Strategies of War
   d. 1990 Clean Air Act

12. The Program (or Project) Evaluation and Review Technique, commonly abbreviated _____, is a model for project management designed to analyze and represent the tasks involved in completing a given project.

_____ is a method to analyze the involved tasks in completing a given project, specially the time needed to complete each task, and identifying the minimum time needed to complete the total project.

_____ was developed primarily to simplify the planning and scheduling of large and complex projects.

   a. 28-hour day
   b. 1990 Clean Air Act
   c. 33 Strategies of War
   d. PERT

13. A _____ is, in some cases, the same as a project manager. _____s are considered to be Project Managers but with engineering qualifications.

Government organizations might have a Senior _____ at the top of the ladder followed by _____ followed by Project Manager.

   a. Critical Chain Project Management
   b. Precedence diagram
   c. Work package
   d. Project engineer

14. _____ is the state or fact of exclusive rights and control over property, which may be an object, land/real estate or intellectual property. An _____ right is also referred to as title. The concept of _____ has existed for thousands of years and in all cultures.

Chapter 17. Managing Projects

a. A4e
b. A Stake in the Outcome
c. Emanation of the state
d. Ownership

15. The _____, is a mathematically based algorithm for scheduling a set of project activities. It is an important tool for effective project management.

It was developed in the 1950s by the Dupont Corporation at about the same time that General Dynamics and the US Navy were developing the Program Evaluation and Review Technique (PERT) Today, it is commonly used with all forms of projects, including construction, software development, research projects, product development, engineering, and plant maintenance, among others.

a. 1990 Clean Air Act
b. 33 Strategies of War
c. 28-hour day
d. Critical path method

16. _____ is one of the managerial functions like planning, organizing, staffing and directing. It is an important function because it helps to check the errors and to take the corrective action so that deviation from standards are minimized and stated goals of the organization are achieved in desired manner. According to modern concepts, _____ is a foreseeing action whereas earlier concept of _____ was used only when errors were detected. _____ in management means setting standards, measuring actual performance and taking corrective action.

a. Decision tree pruning
b. Schedule of reinforcement
c. Turnover
d. Control

17. A _____ in project management and systems engineering, is a tool used to define and group a project's discrete work elements (or tasks) in a way that helps organize and define the total work scope of the project.

A _____ element may be a product, data, a service, or any combination. A _____ also provides the necessary framework for detailed cost estimating and control along with providing guidance for schedule development and control.

a. 28-hour day
b. 33 Strategies of War
c. 1990 Clean Air Act
d. Work breakdown structure

18. A _____ is a graph (flow chart) depicting the sequence in which a project's terminal elements are to be completed by showing terminal elements and their dependencies.

The work breakdown structure or the product breakdown structure show the 'part-whole' relations. In contrast, the _____ shows the 'before-after' relations.

a. 28-hour day
b. 33 Strategies of War
c. 1990 Clean Air Act
d. Project network

19. The _____ (Situation, Task, Action, Result) format is a job interview technique used by interviewers to gather all the relevant information about a specific capability that the job requires. This interview format is said to have a higher degree of predictability of future on-the-job performance than the traditional interview.

- Situation: The interviewer wants you to present a recent challenge and situation in which you found yourself.
- Task: What did you have to achieve? The interviewer will be looking to see what you were trying to achieve from the situation.
- Action: What did you do? The interviewer will be looking for information on what you did, why you did it and what were the alternatives.
- Results: What was the outcome of your actions? What did you achieve through your actions and did you meet your objectives. What did you learn from this experience and have you used this learning since?

a. Rasch models
b. Star
c. Phrase completion
d. Competency-based job descriptions

20. The phrase _____, according to the Organization for Economic Co-operation and Development, refers to 'creative work undertaken on a systematic basis in order to increase the stock of knowledge, including knowledge of man, culture and society, and the use of this stock of knowledge to devise new applications [sic]'

Chapter 17. Managing Projects

New product design and development is more than often a crucial factor in the survival of a company. In an industry that is fast changing, firms must continually revise their design and range of products. This is necessary due to continuous technology change and development as well as other competitors and the changing preference of customers.

   a. 1990 Clean Air Act
   b. Research and development
   c. 33 Strategies of War
   d. 28-hour day

21. A _____ is a type of bar chart that illustrates a project schedule. _____s illustrate the start and finish dates of the terminal elements and summary elements of a project. Terminal elements and summary elements comprise the work breakdown structure of the project.
   a. 1990 Clean Air Act
   b. 33 Strategies of War
   c. 28-hour day
   d. Gantt chart

22. In economics, business, retail, and accounting, a _____ is the value of money that has been used up to produce something, and hence is not available for use anymore. In economics, a _____ is an alternative that is given up as a result of a decision. In business, the _____ may be one of acquisition, in which case the amount of money expended to acquire it is counted as _____.
   a. Cost allocation
   b. Cost
   c. Fixed costs
   d. Cost overrun

23. _____ is a Japanese philosophy that focuses on continuous improvement throughout all aspects of life. When applied to the workplace, _____ activities continually improve all functions of a business, from manufacturing to management and from the CEO to the assembly line workers. By improving standardized activities and processes, _____ aims to eliminate waste .
   a. Sensitivity analysis
   b. Cross-docking
   c. Psychological pricing
   d. Kaizen

Chapter 17. Managing Projects

24. _____ is a business management strategy aimed at embedding awareness of quality in all organizational processes. _____ has been widely used in manufacturing, education, hospitals, call centers, government, and service industries, as well as NASA space and science programs.

As defined by the International Organization for Standardization (ISO):

'_____ is a management approach for an organization, centered on quality, based on the participation of all its members and aiming at long-term success through customer satisfaction, and benefits to all members of the organization and to society.' ISO 8402:1994

One major aim is to reduce variation from every process so that greater consistency of effort is obtained. (Royse, D., Thyer, B., Padgett D., ' Logan T., 2006)

   a. 1990 Clean Air Act
   b. Quality management
   c. 28-hour day
   d. Total quality management

25. _____ can be considered to have three main components: quality control, quality assurance and quality improvement. _____ is focused not only on product quality, but also the means to achieve it. _____ therefore uses quality assurance and control of processes as well as products to achieve more consistent quality.
   a. Total quality management
   b. Quality management
   c. 28-hour day
   d. 1990 Clean Air Act

26. A _____ is a type of business entity in which partners (owners) share with each other the profits or losses of the business. _____s are often favored over corporations for taxation purposes, as the _____ structure does not generally incur a tax on profits before it is distributed to the partners (i.e. there is no dividend tax levied.) However, depending on the _____ structure and the jurisdiction in which it operates, owners of a _____ may be exposed to greater personal liability than they would as shareholders of a corporation.
   a. Mediation
   b. Federal Employers Liability Act
   c. Partnership
   d. Due process

27. _____ is one of the four elements of marketing mix. An organization or set of organizations (go-betweens) involved in the process of making a product or service available for use or consumption by a consumer or business user.

The other three parts of the marketing mix are product, pricing, and promotion.

Chapter 17. Managing Projects

a. Job creation programs
b. Distribution
c. Matching theory
d. Missing completely at random

28. In probability theory and statistics, the _____ or Gaussian distribution is a continuous probability distribution that describes data that clusters around a mean or average. The graph of the associated probability density function is bell-shaped, with a peak at the mean, and is known as the Gaussian function or bell curve.

The _____ can be used to describe, at least approximately, any variable that tends to cluster around the mean.

a. Histogram
b. Generalized normal distribution
c. Heteroskedastic
d. Normal distribution

29. The '_____ scheme' is an economic term, referring to the use of commodity storage for economic stabilization. Specifically, commodities are bought and stored when there is a surplus in the economy and they are sold from these stores when there are shortages in the economy. The institutional buying, storing and selling of commodities by a large player (e.g. a government) can take place for one commodity or a 'basket of commodities'.

a. Reservation wage
b. Power
c. Contingent employment
d. Buffer stock

30. _____ is an American writer on business management practices, best-known for, In Search of Excellence (co-authored with Robert H. Waterman, Jr.)

Peters was born in Baltimore, Maryland. He went to Severn School for High School and attended Cornell University, receiving a bachelor's degree in civil engineering in 1965, and a master's degree in 1966.

a. Adam Smith
b. Abraham Harold Maslow
c. Affiliation
d. Thomas J. Peters

31. _____, widely known as F. W. Taylor, was an American mechanical engineer who sought to improve industrial efficiency. He is regarded as the father of scientific management, and was one of the first management consultants.

Taylor was one of the intellectual leaders of the Efficiency Movement and his ideas, broadly conceived, were highly influential in the Progressive Era.

a. Jonah Jacob Goldberg
b. Geoffrey Colvin
c. Douglas N. Daft
d. Frederick Winslow Taylor

ANSWER KEY

Chapter 1
1. d   2. a   3. d   4. d   5. c   6. d   7. d   8. b   9. d   10. c
11. a   12. b   13. a   14. c   15. c   16. d   17. c   18. d   19. a   20. d
21. c   22. c

Chapter 2
1. b   2. d   3. c   4. d   5. d   6. c   7. d   8. d   9. d   10. d
11. a   12. d   13. c   14. b   15. b   16. d   17. d   18. c   19. b   20. d
21. a   22. d   23. d   24. d   25. d   26. c   27. b   28. d   29. d   30. c
31. d

Chapter 3
1. c   2. c   3. c   4. d   5. a   6. a   7. d   8. d   9. d   10. c
11. a   12. d   13. d   14. d   15. d   16. d   17. d

Chapter 4
1. a   2. d   3. c   4. a   5. c   6. d   7. d   8. b   9. d   10. d
11. c   12. d   13. d   14. d   15. a   16. c   17. c   18. c   19. b   20. d
21. d

Chapter 5
1. d   2. d   3. a   4. a   5. d   6. c   7. c   8. d   9. d   10. d

Chapter 6
1. a   2. b   3. c   4. d   5. c   6. d   7. b   8. d   9. a   10. a
11. d   12. d   13. d   14. b   15. d   16. c   17. d   18. b   19. a   20. d
21. d   22. d   23. b   24. d   25. d

Chapter 7
1. d   2. b   3. d   4. d   5. b   6. b   7. d   8. b   9. d   10. d
11. c   12. d   13. d   14. d   15. a   16. d   17. c   18. b   19. a   20. b
21. d   22. d   23. a   24. d   25. a   26. b   27. b   28. b   29. b   30. b

Chapter 8
1. d   2. d   3. d   4. d   5. b   6. c   7. d   8. d   9. d   10. c
11. d   12. d   13. d   14. b   15. c   16. b   17. d   18. c   19. c   20. d
21. a   22. d   23. d   24. d   25. d   26. c   27. d   28. d   29. c   30. d
31. c   32. d   33. d   34. d   35. b

Chapter 9
1. d   2. c   3. a   4. c   5. b   6. d   7. a   8. b   9. d   10. c
11. c   12. d   13. d   14. c   15. d   16. a   17. b   18. c   19. d   20. d
21. d   22. d   23. d

ANSWER KEY

Chapter 10
1. d   2. a   3. b   4. b   5. d   6. a   7. c   8. b   9. d   10. c
11. a   12. a   13. d   14. c   15. d   16. b   17. b   18. c   19. a   20. a
21. d   22. d   23. d

Chapter 11
1. d   2. b   3. d   4. d   5. a   6. b   7. a   8. d   9. b   10. a
11. d   12. a   13. d   14. a   15. a

Chapter 12
1. d   2. d   3. a   4. c   5. a   6. b   7. c   8. d   9. d   10. d
11. d   12. a   13. d   14. c   15. d   16. c   17. c   18. a   19. d   20. a
21. d   22. d   23. c   24. c   25. d   26. d   27. d

Chapter 13
1. d   2. d   3. d   4. d   5. d   6. d   7. d   8. d   9. c   10. a
11. c   12. c   13. b   14. d   15. d   16. a   17. d   18. a   19. c   20. a
21. d   22. b   23. a   24. d   25. d   26. a   27. a   28. b   29. d

Chapter 14
1. d   2. d   3. c   4. c   5. a   6. a   7. c   8. c   9. c   10. b
11. b   12. b   13. b

Chapter 15
1. d   2. d   3. b   4. d   5. a   6. d

Chapter 16
1. a   2. d   3. a   4. b   5. a   6. c   7. d   8. d   9. d   10. a
11. b   12. a   13. c   14. d   15. a   16. a   17. d

Chapter 17
1. d   2. a   3. c   4. d   5. c   6. d   7. d   8. c   9. d   10. a
11. a   12. d   13. d   14. d   15. d   16. d   17. d   18. d   19. b   20. b
21. d   22. b   23. d   24. d   25. b   26. c   27. b   28. d   29. d   30. d
31. d

www.ingramcontent.com/pod-product-compliance
Lightning Source LLC
Chambersburg PA
CBHW082045230426
43670CB00016B/2788